EXCEL 2003

STEPHEN COPESTAKE

In easy steps is an imprint of Computer Step
Southfield Road . Southam
Warwickshire CV47 0FB . United Kingdom
www.ineasysteps.com

Notice of Liability

Every effort has been made to ensure that this book contains accurate and current information. However, Computer Step and the author shall not be liable for any loss or damage suffered by readers as a result of any information contained herein.

Trademarks

Microsoft® and Windows® are registered trademarks of Microsoft Corporation. All other trademarks are acknowledged as belonging to their respective companies.

Printed and bound in the United Kingdom

ISBN 1-84078-266-8

Contents

Getting started

This chapter will quickly get you up-and-running with Excel. You'll learn about Excel's screen and the terminology it uses, then work with and customize toolbars. You'll enter simple data, learn how to select it then navigate through worksheets. You'll go on to use Office Online to get help with problems and access to lots of great "added-value" features. You'll also get answers to questions via Excel's inbuilt HELP system. Finally, you'll enhance your use of Excel with Quick File Switching, error repair and copying/pasting multiple items.

Covers

Chapter One

The Excel 2003 screen

Below is a detailed illustration of the Excel 2003 screen:

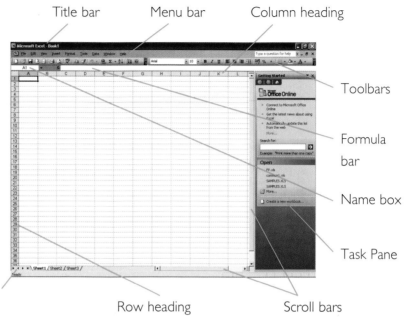

Title bar   Menu bar   Column heading

Toolbars

Formula bar

Name box

Task Pane

Row heading   Scroll bars

This is the worksheet Tab area. The screen components here are used to move between Excel worksheets. See page 19.

Some of these screen components can be hidden at will.

Specifying which screen components display

Pull down the Tools menu and click Options. Then:

Click View

You can have Excel display formulas (rather than their values) globally within cells. This is a useful feature in moderation. Just check Formulas under Window options.

You can also hide sheet tabs, though doing so may possibly decrease worksheet functionality. Uncheck Sheet tabs.

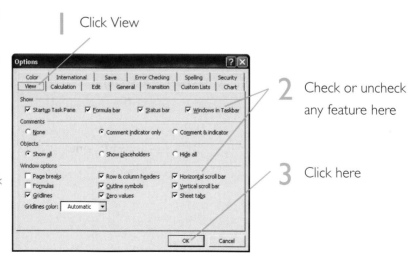

2 Check or uncheck any feature here

3 Click here

Screen components deconstructed

Many Excel screen components are standard to most Windows programs. Some, however, are specialized:

The Formula Bar

This displays the location and contents of the currently selected cell. The Formula Bar represents a particularly useful way to enter:

- formulas

- other cell data (e.g. text)

Column headings

Column headings define each cell within a given column horizontally. Columns are labeled A, B, C, etc.

Row headings

Row headings define each cell within a given row vertically. Rows are numbered 1, 2, 3, etc.

The vertical and horizontal scroll bars

These have some slightly different applications in Excel. First, they enable you to move the visible window vertically up and down the worksheet or horizontally to the left and right, under the control of the mouse. However, for how to use the vertical and horizontal scroll bars in other ways to navigate through Excel 2003 worksheets, see page 18.

Sheet tabs

These enable you to select which spreadsheet should be displayed. By clicking on a sheet tab, you jump to the relevant sheet.

(You can also use sheet tabs to perform operations on more than one worksheet at a time.)

The Task Pane

The Task Pane is a specialized task-based toolbar which now also incorporates the Research pane.

Toolbars

To add a new button to a toolbar or menu, see page 186.

Toolbars are important components in Excel 2003. A toolbar is an on-screen bar which contains shortcut buttons. These symbolize and allow easy access to often-used commands which would normally have to be invoked via one or more menus.

For example, Excel 2003's Standard toolbar lets you:

- create, open, save and print worksheets

- perform copy & paste and cut & paste operations

- undo editing actions

- access Excel's HELP system

You can create your own toolbar. In the Customize dialog (see the above tip), select the Toolbars tab and hit New. Name the toolbar and allocate a template.

by simply clicking on the relevant button.

We'll be looking at toolbars in more detail as we encounter them. For the moment, some general advice:

Specifying which toolbars are displayed

| Choose View, Toolbars

You can't rename any of the toolbars that come with Excel.

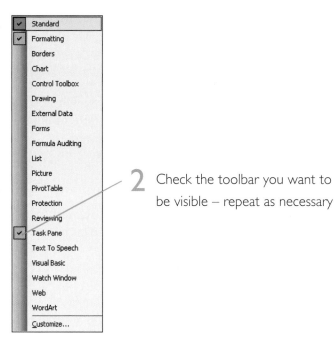

The Task Pane is a toolbar. To hide or show it, uncheck or check the Task Pane entry on the right.

2 Check the toolbar you want to be visible – repeat as necessary

Automatic customization

Menus and toolbars are personalized in Excel 2003.

Submenus aren't customized.

Personalized menus

When you first use Excel 2003, its menus display the features which Microsoft believes are used 95% of the time and features which are infrequently used are not immediately visible. This makes for less cluttered screens.

Personalizing menus is made clear in the illustrations below:

Excel menus expand automatically, after a slight delay. However, to expand them manually, click the chevrons at the bottom of the menu.

Excel 2003's Tools menu, as it first appears...

Automatic customization also applies to toolbars. Note the following:

- *if possible, they display on a single row*
- *they overlap when there isn't enough room on-screen*
- *icons are "promoted" and "demoted" like menu entries*
- *demoted icons are shown in a separate fly-out, reached by clicking:*

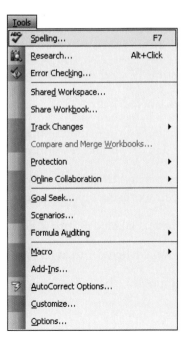

...the expanded menu. (As you use Excel, individual features are dynamically promoted or demoted. This means menus are continually evolving)

Basic terminology

Here, we explore some of the basic terms used throughout Excel.

Worksheets

"Worksheet" is Excel's name for a spreadsheet. Worksheets are arrays of cells used to store data. This often involves simple math calculations linking the cells together in tables, usually for some kind of analysis.

Worksheets are the essential building-blocks of workbooks.

By default, Excel workbooks contain three worksheets: Sheet 1, Sheet 2 and Sheet 3.

Workbooks

A workbook is a file which holds together a collection of worksheets (and possibly charts – see Chapter 14). It will be seen in later chapters that it is usual to have several worksheets linked together and often convenient to summarize the data on these worksheets in the form of associated charts or graphs.

When you create a new document in Excel, you're actually creating a new workbook. Each new workbook has a default name: Book 1, Book 2 etc.

See Chapter 4 for more information on workbooks.

The worksheet window

The opening Excel 2003 window displays (if the Task Pane is not visible):

*   12 columns labeled A thru L

*   28 rows labeled 1 thru 28

The exact number of rows and columns shown depends on the screen size, video driver and resolution.

It must be appreciated that this is only the extreme top left-hand corner. The full worksheet extends to:

*   256 columns labeled A thru Z then AA thru IV

*   65,536 rows labeled 1 thru 65,536

This means each worksheet contains 16,777,216 cells. See the illustration on the facing page for further clarification.

As we've just seen, the Excel 2003 screen displays only a tiny section of the available worksheet. The illustration below displays this graphically:

This area covers the cell range A1 to I18.

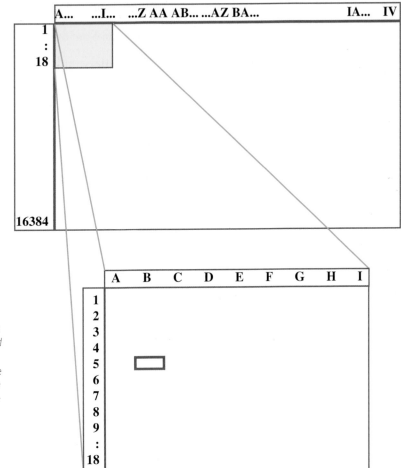

The location (or "address") of a cell is given by its column letter and row number, e.g. the cell at the intersection of the second column and the fifth row (as here) is given the address or cell reference B5.

The yellow section – only a tiny part of the overall worksheet – is shown in its overall context in the lower half of the illustration.

Keying in data

In Excel 2003, you can enter the following basic data types:

- values (numbers) or dates (separate components by - or /) or times (e.g. **6.45a** for 6.45 a.m. or **3.55p** for 3.55 p.m.)

- text (e.g. headings and explanatory material)

- math functions (e.g. Sine or Cosine)

- formulas (combinations of values, text and functions)

You can use two techniques to enter data into any cell in a worksheet.

Entering data directly

Excel 2003 lets you insert and work with Euros. To insert the Euro symbol, hold down Alt and type 0128 on the Numerical keypad to the right of your keyboard. Release Alt.

First, move the mouse pointer over any cell and left-click once. Alternatively, you can also use the keyboard to target a cell: simply move the cell pointer with the cursor keys until it's over the relevant cell. Whichever method you use, Excel 2003 surrounds the active cell with a border.

The principal fonts that support the Euro are Courier, Tahoma, Times and Arial.

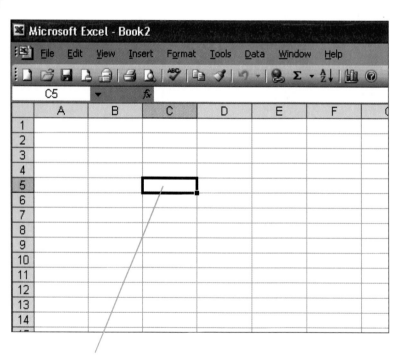

Active cell

When you enter values which are too big (physically) to fit in the holding cell, Excel 2003 may insert an error message.

To resolve this, widen the column. Or pull down the Format menu and click Column, Autofit Selection to have Excel automatically increase the column size to match the contents.

Although you can enter data *directly* into a cell (by simply clicking in the cell and typing it in), there's another method you can use which is often easier. Excel provides a special screen component known as the Formula Bar.

The illustration below shows the end of a blank worksheet. Some sample text has been inserted into cell IV65536 (note that the Name box tells you which cell is currently active).

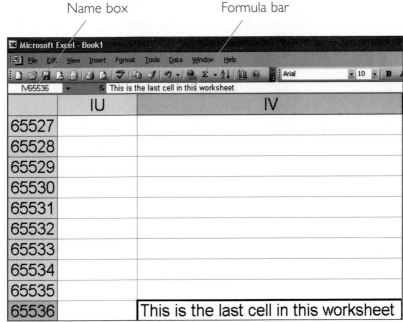

You can enter the same data into more than one cell. Select the cells then type in the data. Hit Ctrl+Enter.

If you start to enter alphanumeric data in a cell and Excel determines that it matches data already present in that column, it fills in the remaining data for you. Hit Enter to accept the suggestion.

Entering data via the Formula bar

Click the cell you want to insert data into. Then click the Formula bar. Type in the data. Then follow step 1 below. If you decide not to proceed with the operation, follow step 2 instead:

2 Click here (or press Esc)

X ✓ ƒx This is the last cell in this worksheet

Click here (or press Enter)

Selection techniques

You can also use this technique. Place the cell pointer in the first cell. Press F8 – "EXT" appears in the Status bar. Use the cursor keys to define the selection. Finally, press F8 again.

Before you can carry out any editing operations on cells in Excel, you have to select them first. Selecting a single cell is very easy: you merely click in it. However, Excel provides a variety of selection techniques which you can use to select more than one cell.

Selecting adjacent cell ranges

The easiest way to do this is to use the mouse. Click in the first cell in the range; hold down the left mouse button and drag over the remaining cells. Release the mouse button.

You can use the keyboard, too. Select the first cell in the range. Hold down one Shift key as you use the relevant cursor key to extend the selection. Release the keys when the correct selection has been defined.

Selecting separate cell ranges

Excel lets you select more than one range at a time:

A useful shortcut that needs a bit of practice. Select one or more cell ranges then hold down Shift. Click the last cell you want in the selection – Excel selects all cells between the first selected cell and the one you just clicked.

In the example (and ignoring the selections on the right of the illustration), if you selected A14:B17 first and then selected A4:B6, Shift-clicking B15 would select A4:B17 . . .

Selected ranges (cells, except the first, are see-through,

so you can view changes to underlying data)

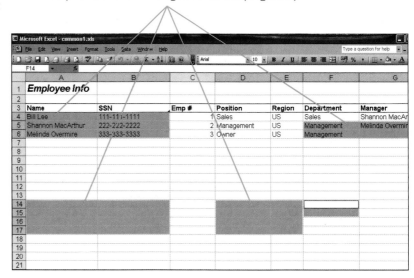

To select joint ranges, select the first in the normal way (you can only use the mouse method here). Then hold down Ctrl as you select subsequent ranges.

Groups of adjacent cells are known as "ranges" in Excel. Ranges are described in terms of their upper-left and lower-right cell references (with each separated by a colon).

For example, the range beginning with cell D3 and ending with H16 would be shown as: D3:H16.

Selecting a single row or column

To select every cell within a row or column automatically, click the row or column heading.

Column heading

Row heading

Non-adjacent ranges are separated by commas e.g. A3:B9,D3:H16.

Selecting multiple rows or columns

To select more than one row or column, click a row or column heading. Hold down the left mouse button and drag to select adjacent rows or columns.

Selecting an entire worksheet

Carry out step 1 below:

Click the Select All button (or hit Ctrl+A)

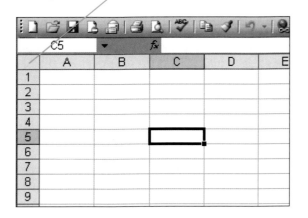

Moving around in worksheets

Excel 2003 facilitates worksheet navigation. As you move the insertion point from cell to cell, the relevant row and column headers are highlighted.

Using the keyboard

1 Use the cursor keys to move one cell left, right, up or down

2 Hold down Ctrl as you use 1. above; this jumps to the edge of the current section (e.g. if cell B11 is active and you hold down Ctrl as you press the right cursor, Excel jumps to IV11)

3 Press Home to jump to the first cell in the active row, or Ctrl+Home to move to A1

4 Press Page Up or Page Down to move up or down by 1 screen

5 Press Alt+Page Down to move one screen to the right, or Alt+Page Up to move one screen to the left

Using the scroll bars

1 To scroll quickly to another section of the active worksheet, drag the scroll box along the scroll bar until you reach it (hold down Shift to speed it up)

2 To move one window to the left or right, click to the left or right of the scroll box in the horizontal scroll bar

3 To move one window up or down, click above or below the scroll box in the vertical scroll bar

4 To move up or down by one row, click the arrows in the vertical scroll bar

5 To move left or right by one column, click the arrows in the horizontal scroll bar

Using the Go To dialog

1 Hit F5

2 In the Go To dialog, type in a cell reference (its positional identification e.g. H23) or a cell range (e.g. J25:K36) then click OK

Switching between worksheets

Because workbooks have more than one worksheet, Excel provides two easy and convenient methods for moving between them.

Using the Tab area

You can use the Tab area (at the base of the Excel screen – see page 8) to:

When you click a worksheet tab, Excel 2003 emboldens the name and makes the tab background white.

- jump to the first or last sheet

- jump to the next or previous sheet

- jump to a specific sheet

See the illustration below:

You can "color-code" worksheet tabs, for ease of reference. Right-click a tab and select Tab Color in the shortcut menu. Select a color and then click OK.

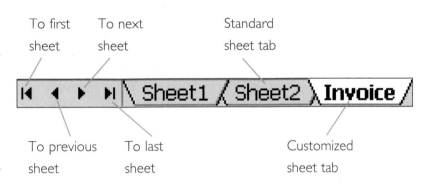

To first sheet | To next sheet | Standard sheet tab

To previous sheet | To last sheet | Customized sheet tab

You can enter or amend data in more than one worksheet at a time: just select multiple worksheet tabs and make the changes. However, don't forget that data may be replaced in the process.

To move to a specific sheet, simply click the relevant tab.

An example: in the illustration above, to jump to the "Invoice" worksheet, simply click the appropriate tab.

Using the keyboard

1 Hit Ctrl+Page Up to move to the previous worksheet tab

2 Hit Ctrl+Page Down to move to the next worksheet tab

Using the Watch Window

You can use the Watch Window to track cells (often those containing formulas) while you're working on another part of the same or another sheet, or even in another workbook. The Watch Window is a great labor-saving device: it stops you having to continually switch between worksheets and workbooks.

Using the Watch Window

1 Select the cell(s) you want to watch

2 Choose Tools, Formula Auditing, Show Watch Window

To remove a cell from the Watch Window, select its entry and click Delete Watch.

3 Click Add Watch

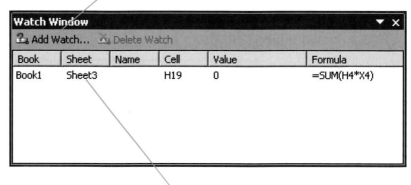

If the Watch Window has entries that refer to another workbook, they only display if the other workbook is currently open.

5 To view a cell, double-click its entry

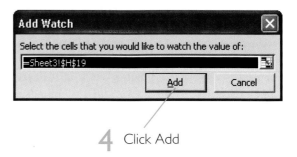

4 Click Add

Quick File Switching

In the past, only programs (not individual windows within programs) displayed on the Windows Taskbar. With Excel 2003, however, all open windows display as separate buttons.

In the following example, four new worksheets have been created in Excel 2003. All four display as separate windows, although only one copy of Excel 2003 is running:

Four Excel 2003 windows

This is clarified by a glance at Excel 2003's Window menu which (as before) shows all open Excel windows:

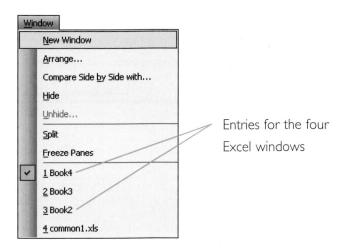

Entries for the four Excel windows

1   To go to a worksheet window, simply click its Taskbar button

2   Find Quick File Switching annoying? No problem. To disable it, choose Tools, Options. Select the View tab and uncheck Windows in Taskbar

Repairing errors

Excel 2003 provides a special feature you can use to repair its installation.

Detect and Repair

Detect and Repair fixes Registry errors and missing files; it will not repair damaged worksheets. If the process doesn't work, reinstall Excel 2003.

Do the following to correct program errors (but note selecting "Discard my customized settings and restore default settings" in step 2 will ensure that all default Excel settings are restored, so any you've customized – including menu/toolbar positions and view settings – will be lost):

1 Choose Help, Detect and Repair

2 Select one or both options

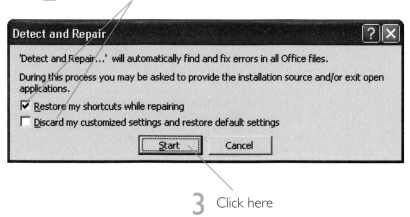

Detect and Repair

'Detect and Repair...' will automatically find and fix errors in all Office files.

During this process you may be asked to provide the installation source and/or exit open applications.

☑ Restore my shortcuts while repairing

☐ Discard my customized settings and restore default settings

Start   Cancel

3 Click here

You can use another method to repair damaged files. Press Ctrl+O. In the open dialog, highlight the corrupt file and click the drop-down arrow on the Open button. In the menu, click Open and Repair. (Excel may run this procedure automatically when errors are detected.)

4 Follow the on-screen instructions – Detect and Repair can be a lengthy process

5 You may have to re-enter your user name and initials when you restart your Office applications

...cont'd

You can also use a further procedure for instances when Excel "hangs" (ceases to respond).

Application Recovery

When errors occur, Excel should give you the option of saving open files before it closes.

1 Click Start, All Programs, Microsoft Office, Microsoft Office Tools, Microsoft Office Application Recovery

2 Select the program which isn't responding

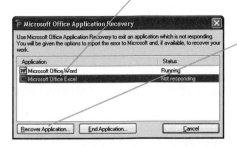

You should make sure AutoRecover is turned on to make it easier to recover worksheets. See page 63.

3 Click Recover Application to have Excel try to recover the workbook(s) you were working on

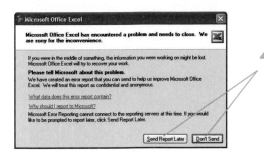

4 Decide whether to email error details to Microsoft

Workbooks with [Recovered] against them are usually more recent than those with [Original] in the title.

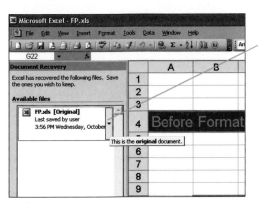

5 Excel opens. Click the file you want to keep (usually the most recent) then select Open or View to view it or Save As to save it

This is the Document Recovery Task Pane – when you've finished with it, click the Close button.

Collect and Paste

You can copy multiple items to the Office Clipboard from within any Windows program which supports copy-and-paste but you can only paste in the last one.

If you want to copy-and-paste multiple items of text and/or pictures into a worksheet, you can now copy as many as 24 items. These are stored in a special version of the Windows Clipboard called the Office Clipboard that in turn is located in the Task Pane. The Office Clipboard displays a visual representation of the data.

Using the Office Clipboard

Use standard procedures to copy multiple examples of data and/or pictures – after the first copy, the Clipboard should appear in the Task Pane. Then:

To call up the Office Clipboard at any time, pull down the Edit menu and click Office Clipboard.

1 Click the data you want to insert – it appears at the insertion point

If the Clipboard Task Pane persistently refuses to appear after pasting, call it up manually and hit the Options button. Check Show Office Clipboard Automatically.

You must use the technique shown here to paste from the Office Clipboard: the normal paste commands like Ctrl+V only paste from the standard Windows Clipboard.

2 If you're inserting text, a Smart Tag appears (see the facing page)

3 To clear the contents of the Office Clipboard, click the Clear All button (or close Excel and any other Office modules you may be running at the time)

Smart Tags

Excel 2003 recognizes certain types of data and flags them with a purple triangle in the relevant cell. When you move the mouse pointer over the triangle, an "action button" appears that provides access to commands that would otherwise have to be accessed from menus/toolbars or even other programs. Smart Tags are data-specific labels.

There are several types of Smart Tag in Excel 2003. These include Person Names from Outlook Contact lists or from email recipients and financial symbols.

Using Smart Tags

1 When the triangle appears, click here

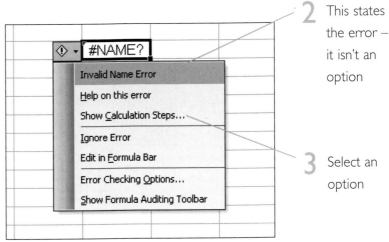

2 This states the error – it isn't an option

3 Select an option

Excel also uses additional action buttons that resemble Smart Tags in the way they work.

The Insert Options button

Other action buttons include AutoCorrect.

1 "Button" has been copied and the Paste command (Shift+Insert) issued...

2 Clicking the arrow launches a menu – make a choice

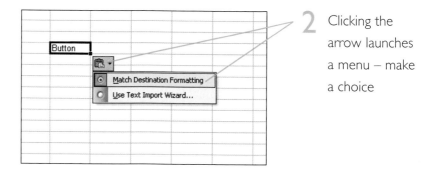

The AutoFill button

1 Carry out an AutoFill operation – see page 36 for more information

2 Clicking the arrow launches a menu – make a choice

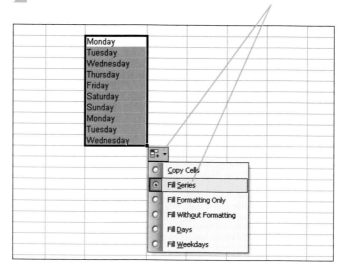

Using Office Online

Imagine a scenario. You're sitting at your desk, working on an Excel spreadsheet, when you hit a problem. What do you do (apart from not panicking)? The answer is, you use Office Online to find the answer you need.

Office Online is a special website which provides dedicated resources that are updated regularly in line with user feedback. There are links to Office Online in various of the Task Panes and menus you'll meet as you work thru this book. Office Online gives you helpful articles, templates, clips and training links.

Connecting to Office Online

The Getting Started Task Pane launches when you start Excel 2003. If it doesn't, hit Ctrl+F1 then select it in the drop-down list

A lot of the help that Microsoft provides is only available on the Web, so it pays to use Office Online.

2 With your Internet connection live, click here

Office Online has several key areas. Use the following as guides (Office Online may have changed when you read this):

- *Assistance – hints and tips. Also Excel-specific help*
- *Training – links to tutorials*
- *Templates – lots of templates and some downloads*
- *Clip Art and Media – clips organized under headings*
- *Downloads – access to popular downloads and a link to Windows Update*
- *Office Marketplace – showcases non-Microsoft products and services*
- *Product Information – additional services*

3 Select an area then any link

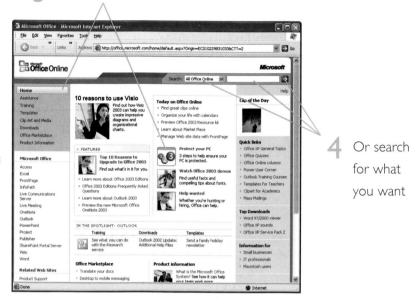

4 Or search for what you want

5 If you carried out a search, click a link

Getting help from within Excel

Type in your question in the Ask a Question box and press Enter

If you'd rather use Office Online directly to get help, you can hide the Ask a Question box to make more room onscreen. Choose Tools, Customize. Right-click the box and uncheck "Show Ask a Question box". Hit Close.

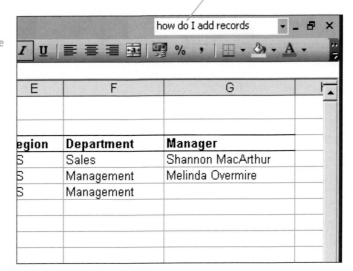

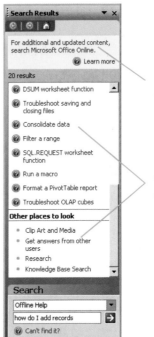

3   Or power up your Web connection and click here to launch Office Online

2   The Search Results Task Pane launches. Click any relevant entry (especially, click Knowledge Base Search to hunt thru the Microsoft Knowledge Base, a vast repository of problem-solving solutions)

Alternatively, press F1

2 Type in search text (optimally, 2–7 words) then hit the arrow

3 Alternatively, fire up Office Online directly or select a specific link (Assistance, Training and Downloads are Office Online areas. Hit Communities for access to Office-specific forums)

If your Internet connection is live, step 2 searches Office Online.

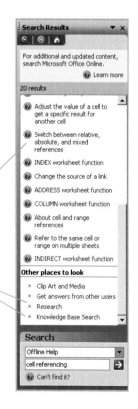

4 After step 2, select a link in the Search Results pane

The Knowledge Base is a vast store of informational material and articles that Microsoft maintains for the benefit of users. You're almost certain to find what you need there.

5 Or hit a suggestion. Try Knowledge Base Search if you need detailed help – Research refers to the Research Task Pane

Worksheet basics

It's important to "forward-plan" worksheets, to ensure they do what you need them to and your data is easy to follow. In this chapter, you'll learn how to do this. We'll also examine the different types of data you can enter and look at how to modify it later. Excel 2003 has numerous features that act as shortcuts to data entry; you'll use these to save time and effort. Then you'll discover how to work with number formats, specify suitable data types, insert formulas into cells and "parse" formulas.

Finally, you'll carry out simple What-If tests, resize rows and columns and insert new cells, rows and columns.

Covers

Chapter Two

Layout planning

When you start Excel 2003, a blank worksheet is automatically created and loaded. This means you can click any cell and start entering data immediately. However, it's a good idea to give some thought to an overall layout strategy before you do this.

Look at the simple worksheet excerpt below:

2	Widgets ordered =		425.00	
3	Price per unit =		$0.73	
4	Amount due (excluding returns)			

Here, the text occupies far more space than the numbers and formulas. The problem has been solved by widening the column containing the text (see page 43 for how to do this). The difficulty is that this method prevents subsequent lines in the column from being subdivided into further columns.

Look at the next illustration:

2	Widgets ordered =		425.00	
3	Price per unit =		$0.73	
4	Amount due (excluding returns)			

This text has bled into the next column

The second method is often the most flexible.

Here, on the other hand, the final text entry has been allowed to straddle as many adjacent columns as necessary. The proviso here is that you must ensure you leave as many empty adjacent cells as are necessary to fully display the text.

1 As you enter data into your worksheet, use the techniques discussed here (and on page 43) to ensure your data is clear and easily comprehensible

2 Ensure your worksheet has an effective overall "look" – see Chapter 12 for more information on how to format worksheets

Data types

To force a sequence of digits to be input as text, precede them by a single quotation mark. If Excel then queries this by launching a Smart Tag, click the button then select Number Stored as Text in the drop-down menu.

(If you don't want Excel to go on querying numbers inserted as text via this technique, choose Tools, Options. Select the Error Checking tab and uncheck Number stored as text.)

In Chapter 1, we looked at how to key in simple data. Now, we'll examine the types of data you can enter in more detail.

Excel 2003 determines the type of data entered into a cell by the sequence of characters keyed. The types are:

- numbers (i.e. digits, decimal point, #, %, +, –)

- text (any other string of characters)

- formulas (always preceded by =)

The worksheet excerpt below shows these data types in action:

These are default alignments. To apply a new alignment, select the cell(s). Right-click over them. In the menu, click Format Cells. In the Format Cells dialog, click the Alignment tab. Select a new alignment. Click OK.

B2 contains text (aligned to the left of the cell)

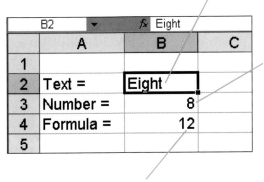

B3 contains the number 8 (aligned to the right of the cell)

B4 contains the hidden formula: =8+4

2 To view the formula instead of the result, hit Ctrl+` (the ` character resides at the top left of the keyboard, under the function keys)

When a formula has been inserted into a cell, Excel 2003 evaluates it. The resultant value – in the case of B4 above, 12 – is shown, aligned to the right.

For more information on formulas, see pages 39–41.

Modifying existing data

You can amend the contents of a cell in two ways:

- via the Formula bar

- from within the cell

When you use either of these methods, Excel 2003 enters a special state known as Edit Mode.

If in-cell editing doesn't work, pull down the Tools menu and click Options. Select the Edit tab, then check Edit directly in cell. Finally, click OK.

Amending existing data using the Formula bar

Click the cell whose contents you want to change. Then click in the Formula bar. Make the appropriate revisions and/or additions. Then press Enter. Excel updates the relevant cell.

To undo or redo any editing action, press Ctrl+Z or Ctrl+Y.

Amending existing data internally

Click the cell whose contents you want to change. Press F2. Make the appropriate revisions and/or additions *within the cell*. Then press Enter.

The illustration below shows a section from a blank workbook:

The way Excel actually displays data in cells depends on the number format applied – see page 37.

Also crucial are the Windows XP Regional settings (Control Panel, Regional and Language Options – Regional Options tab).

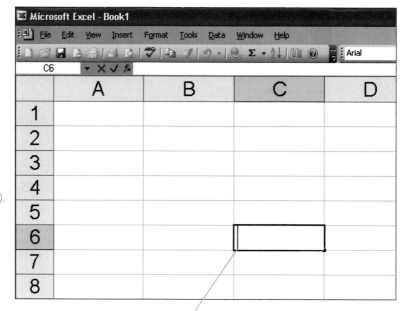

Cell C6 in Edit Mode (note the flashing insertion point)

AutoComplete

Excel 2003 has a range of features which save you time and effort: AutoComplete, AutoFill and AutoCorrect. AutoComplete examines the contents of the active column and tries to anticipate what you're about to type.

1 Enter a series of text values

2 To duplicate any of these entries in the cell immediately below, type in one letter (here "s") to prompt Excel to insert the correct term then hit Enter – this feature isn't case-sensitive

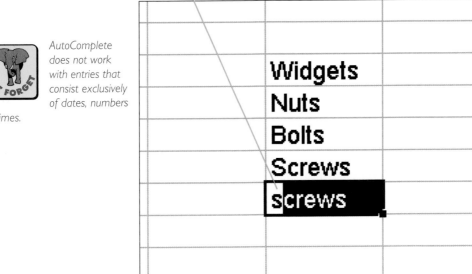

3 Alternatively, right-click over the cell and select Pick From Drop-down List

4 Then click an entry

AutoFill

AutoFill extends formatting and formulas in lists.

Types of series you can use AutoFill to complete include the following:

* *1st Period, 2nd Period, 3rd Period etc.*
* *Mon, Tue, Wed etc.*
* *Quarter 1, Quarter 2, Quarter 3 etc.*
* *Week1, Week2, Week3 etc.*

Data series don't need to contain every possibility. For instance, you could have: "Mon, Thu, Sun, Wed" etc.

Excel 2003 lets you insert data series automatically. This is a very useful and timesaving feature. Look at the illustration below:

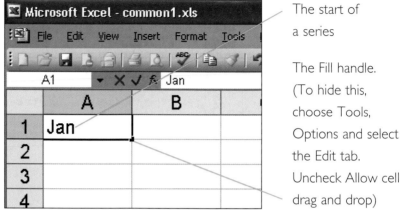

The start of a series

The Fill handle. (To hide this, choose Tools, Options and select the Edit tab. Uncheck Allow cell drag and drop)

If you wanted to insert month names in successive cells in column A, you could do so manually. But there's a much easier way. You can use Excel's AutoFill feature.

Using AutoFill to create a series

1 Type in the first element(s) of the series in consecutive cells then select all the cells

2 Drag the fill handle over the cells into which you want to extend the series (in the example above, A2:A12) – Excel 2003 extrapolates the initial entry or entries into the appropriate series

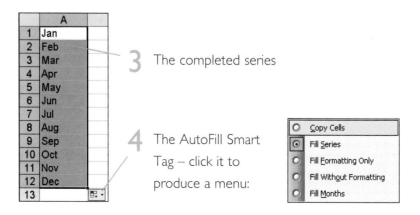

3 The completed series

4 The AutoFill Smart Tag – click it to produce a menu:

Number formats

You can customize the way cell contents (e.g. numbers and dates/times) display in Excel 2003. You can specify:

- at what point numbers are rounded up

- how minus values are displayed (for example, whether they display in red, and/or with "–" in front of them)

- (in the case of currency values) which currency symbol (e.g. $) is used

- (in the case of dates and times) the generic display type (e.g. *month/day/year* or *month/year*)

Available formats are organized under general categories. These include: Number, Currency and Fraction.

Applying a number format

You can create your own number formats. Select Custom in the Category list then apply the formatting you want.

1 Select the cells you want to customize then hit Ctrl+1

Sometimes, you likely will want to enter numbers as text (e.g. a telephone or Social Security number). In this case, choose the Text category.

2 Ensure the Number tab is active

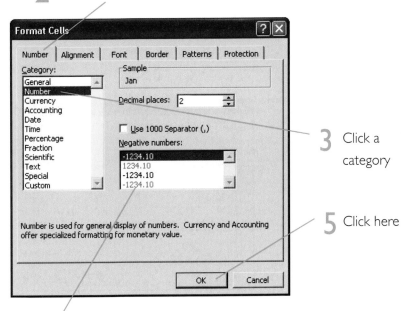

3 Click a category

5 Click here

If a cell has had the Date number format applied, dates appear by default in a specific format. For example, "August 12, 2003" is shown as: 8/12/2003.

To change this, specify a new format in step 4.

4 Complete these options (they vary with the category)

Data validation

You can search for validated cells. Hit F5. Click Special then Data validation, All (selecting Data validation, Same instead finds cells with the same validation setting as the currently selected cell). Hit OK.

You can have Excel 2003 "validate" data. This can mean:

- restricting cells so only data which is within specific number or time limits can be entered

- restricting cells so only a specific number of characters can be entered

Applying data validation

See page 98 for how to trace cells that don't meet their validation targets.

1 Select one or more cells

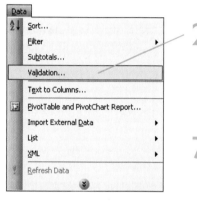

2 Choose Data, Validation

To apply a character limit, select Text Length in step 4. Follow step 5. In step 6, enter min. and max. limits (e.g. "4" and "8"). Carry out step 8.

7 Optionally, hit the Input Message and Error Alert tabs to set data entry and error messages

Re step 5 – you can select from various operators. These include the following:

- *between or not between*
- *equal to or not equal to*
- *greater than or less than*
- *greater than or equal to*
- *less than or equal to*

3 Ensure the Settings tab is active

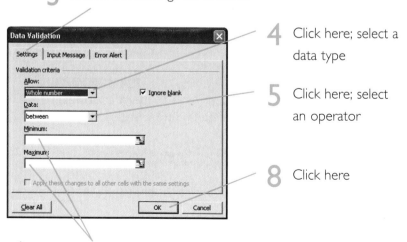

4 Click here; select a data type

5 Click here; select an operator

8 Click here

Hit the Clear All button to remove validation.

6 Specify 1 or 2 limits (values, formulas or cell addresses)

Formulas – an overview

Formulas are cell entries which define how other values relate to each other.

You can use a feature called Range Finder to visually redefine the cells a formula applies to.

When you're creating or editing a formula and Excel surrounds the arguments with a blue border, drag one or more of these to a new cell selection. The formula updates automatically.

As a very simple example, consider the following:

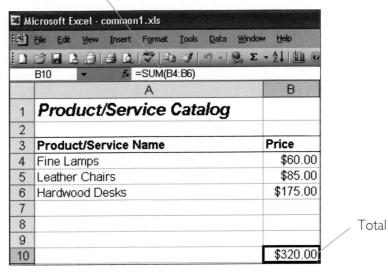

The underlying formula – see below

Total

Here, a cell has been defined which returns the total of cells B4:B6. Obviously, in this instance you could insert the total easily enough yourself because the individual values are so small, and because we're only dealing with a small number of cells. But what happens if the cell values are larger and/or more numerous, or – more to the point – if they're liable to change frequently?

To select cells that contain formulas, pre-select a range (or select a typical cell) then hit F5. Click the Special button and select Formulas. Check the data types you want to select and hit OK.

The answer is to insert a formula which carries out the necessary calculation automatically.

If you look at the Formula bar in the illustration, you'll see the formula which does this:

=SUM(B4:B6)

Many Excel formulas are much more complex than this, but the principles remain the same.

Inserting a formula

All formulas in Excel 2003 begin with an equals sign. This is usually followed by a permutation of the following:

- an operand (cell reference, e.g. B4)

- a function (e.g. the summation function, SUM)

- a math operator (+, –, / and ⋆)

- comparison operators (<, >, <=, >= and =)

Excel supports a very wide range of functions organized into numerous categories. For more information on how to insert functions, see Chapter 6.

The math operators are (in the order in which they appear in the list): *plus*, *minus*, *divide* and *multiply*.

The comparison operators are (in the order in which they appear in the list): *less than*, *greater than*, *less than or equal to*, *greater than or equal to* and *equals*.

There are two ways to enter formulas:

Entering a formula directly into the cell

1 Click a cell then type = followed by your formula. When you've finished, press Enter

Entering a formula into the Formula bar

Click a cell then click in the Formula bar. Type = followed by your formula

2 When you've finished, press Enter

3 Or click here

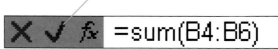

=sum(B4:B6)

The Formula Evaluator

When formulas become complex (as they frequently do), it can be difficult to see how Excel arrives at the eventual result. However, you can use a feature called Formula Evaluator to step sequentially through each calculation.

Using Formula Evaluator

1   Select the cell which contains the formula (you can only evaluate one cell at a time)

2   Choose Tools, Formula Auditing, Evaluate Formula

4   Click Step In to view a linked formula or Step Out to return to the original

The result of the evaluation is shown in italics.

If a reference appears in a formula more than once, the Step In button is only available for the first occurrence. (It isn't available at all if the formula refers to a cell in another workbook.)

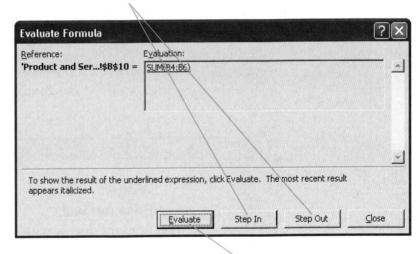

3   Click Evaluate – repeat as often as required

5   Optionally, click Restart to begin over

6   Click Close when you're done

Simple What-If tests

The power of a worksheet is only really appreciated when you carry out "What-If" tests. These involve adjusting the numbers in selected cells in order to observe the effect on formulas throughout the worksheet. Any such changes "ripple through" the worksheet.

In the simple example below, C4 has the following formula:

=C2*C3

which multiplies the contents of C2 by C3.

	A	B	C
1			
2		Widgets ordered =	425
3		Price per unit =	$0.73
4		Amount due (excluding returns)	$310.25

By entering alternative values into C2 or C3, you can watch the changes filter through to C4. In the next illustration, the value in C2 has changed; Excel 2003 has automatically calculated the effect on the total:

	A	B	C
1			
2		Widgets ordered =	562
3		Price per unit =	$0.73
4		Amount due (excluding returns)	$410.26

The change in C2 has cascaded down into the C4 total

Changes you made to data don't produce the relevant update? Pull down the Tools menu and click Options. In the Options dialog, select the Calculation tab and then Automatic

Indigo

Store# 00288 Indigo South Centre
100 Anderson Rd South East
Calgary,AB T2J 3V1
Phone: (403) 225-0033
Fax: (403) 225-0620
* Thank you for shopping at Indigo *
Store# 00288 Term# 005 Trans# 59030
Operator: 704JK 11/28/2006 12:32

iREWARDS SALE
30073522

****

LEARN2 TRAINING FOR MS EXCEL	$14.99G
781735807835	
EXCEL 2003	$13.45G
1840782668	
Original Price $14.95	
iRewards Discount $-1.50	

****

Items 2

Subtotal		$28.44
GST:	6.0%	$1.71
Total:		**$30.15**
CASH:		$50.00
Change		$19.85

****

Your Total Savings: $1.50
Promotions: $0.00
iREWARDS: $1.50

****

Holiday returns accepted until
Jan 14 2007. Items in store bought
condition and returned with a gift
receipt may be exchanged for a
credit note for the value of
the item on the receipt
Store# 00288 Term# 005 Trans# 59030
GST Registration # R897152666

0028800500590301

Si vous n'êtes pas entièrement satisfait d'un de vos achats, n'hésitez pas à le retourner pour un remboursement ou un échange dans un délai de 14 jours. Nous exigeons cependant que l'article soit dans le même état qu'au moment de l'achat et que vous présentiez un reçu provenant d'une de nos librairies. Les articles accompagnés d'un reçu-cadeau et retournés en condition de revente peuvent être échangés ou remboursés par une note de crédit pour la valeur de l'article lors de l'achat. Veuillez noter qu'aucun échange ou remboursement ne sera accepté pour les magazines ou les journaux.

If, for any reason, you purchase an item that is not totally satisfactory, please feel free to return it for refund or exchange within 14 days; we simply ask that the item be returned in store-bought condition and be accompanied by a proof of purchase from any of our stores. Items accompanied by a gift receipt and returned in store-bought condition may be exchanged or refunded onto a credit note for the value of the item at the time of purchase. Please note we cannot provide an exchange or refund of magazines or newspapers.

Si vous n'êtes pas entièrement satisfait d'un de vos achats, n'hésitez pas à le retourner pour un remboursement ou un échange dans un délai de 14 jours. Nous exigeons cependant que l'article soit dans le même état qu'au moment de l'achat et que vous présentiez un reçu provenant d'une de nos librairies. Les articles accompagnés d'un reçu-cadeau et retournés en condition de revente peuvent être échangés ou remboursés par une note de crédit pour la valeur de l'article lors de l'achat. Veuillez noter qu'aucun échange ou remboursement ne sera accepté pour les magazines ou les journaux.

If, for any reason, you purchase an item that is not totally satisfactory, please feel free to return it for refund or exchange within 14 days; we simply ask that the item be returned in store-bought condition and be accompanied by a proof of purchase from any of our stores. Items accompanied by a gift receipt and returned in store-bought condition may be exchanged or refunded onto a credit note for the value of the item at the time of purchase. Please note we cannot provide an exchange or refund of magazines or newspapers.

Si vous n'êtes pas entièrement satisfait d'un de vos achats, n'hésitez pas à le retourner pour un remboursement ou un échange dans un délai de 14 jours. Nous exigeons cependant que l'article soit dans le même état qu'au moment de l'achat et que vous présentiez un reçu provenant d'une de nos librairies. Les articles accompagnés d'un reçu-cadeau et retournés en condition de revente peuvent être échangés ou remboursés par une note de crédit pour la valeur de l'article lors de l'achat et de la livraison

Amending row/column sizes

You can also use a dialog. Select rows or columns then choose Format, Column, Width or Format, Row, Height.

Sooner or later, when there is too much data in cells to display adequately, you'll find it necessary to resize rows or columns.

Changing row height

1. To change one row's height, click the row heading. If you want to change multiple rows, hold down Ctrl and click the appropriate extra headings

Want to have one column's width match another? Click in the column you want to copy and hit Ctrl+C. Select the target column and choose Edit, Paste Special. In the dialog, select Column widths and hit OK.

2. Place the mouse pointer (it changes to a cross) just under the row heading(s) and drag up or down

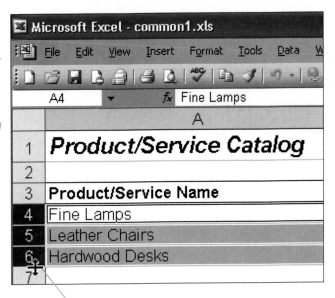

Excel has a useful "Best Fit" feature. When the mouse pointer has changed to the form shown in the illustration, double-click to have the row(s) or column(s) adjust themselves automatically to their contents.

The transformed pointer. Rows 4–6 are being amended

Changing column width

To set a standard column width for all sheets in the active workbook, right-click a sheet tab and hit Select All Sheets. Choose Format, Column, Standard Width. Set a width in the dialog.

1. Follow step 1 above but select one or more column headings

2. Place the mouse pointer (it changes to a cross) to the right of the column heading(s) and drag to the left or right

Inserting cells, rows or columns

You can insert additional cells, rows or columns into worksheets.

If you select cells in more than one row or column, Excel 2003 inserts the equivalent number of new rows or columns.

Inserting a new row or column

First, select one or more cells within the row(s) or column(s) where you want to carry out the insert operation. Now pull down the Insert menu and click Rows or Columns, as appropriate. Excel 2003 inserts the new row(s) or column(s) immediately.

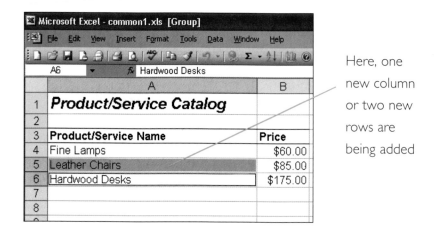

Here, one new column or two new rows are being added

Inserting a new cell range

Select the range where you want to insert the new cells. Pull down the Insert menu and click Cells. Now carry out step 1 or step 2 below. Finally, follow step 3.

1 Click here to have Excel make room for the new cells by moving the selected range *to the right*

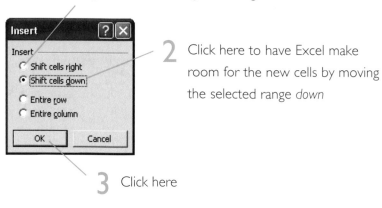

2 Click here to have Excel make room for the new cells by moving the selected range *down*

3 Click here

Copy/move techniques

Copying and moving data are important techniques in Excel: they have specialized applications you don't meet in other programs like word processors. With this chapter, you'll soon be copying data like a pro.

First, you'll copy and move data within worksheets. Then you'll move on to more advanced techniques like copying to other worksheets and workbooks. You'll also perform copy operations that are restricted to specific cell aspects, then use a shortcut that makes copying data to adjacent cells even easier. You'll also move worksheets to a different location within the host workbook and to other workbooks.

Finally, you'll drag-and-drop data directly into Excel 2003 from within Internet Explorer.

Covers

Chapter Three

Copying and moving cells

You can also use AutoFill to copy data. Select a cell range then Ctrl+drag the Fill handle (see page 36) over the adjacent cells you want to copy the data into.

If you use this technique for more than one cell but don't hold down Ctrl (or if you use it for a single cell but do hold down Ctrl), you get a standard AutoFill operation instead (the data is extrapolated, not copied).

Excel 2003 lets you copy or move cells:

- within the same worksheet

- from one worksheet to another

- from one worksheet to another in a different workbook

Copying data within the same worksheet

1 Select a cell range

2 When the mouse pointer changes to an arrow, Ctrl+drag the range to a new location

Copying and moving don't just affect data, they also affect formulas, comments and formatting. Also, any hidden cells are included.

When you copy or move data in cells which contain formulas, Excel adjusts the cell references.

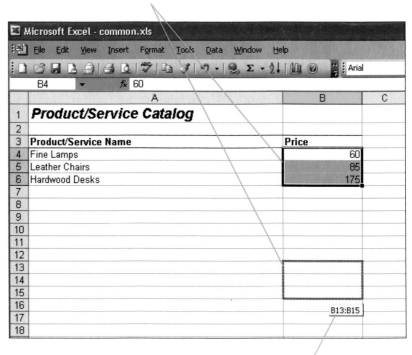

Excel tells you what the new cell address will be – neat, huh?

Want to prevent copied blank cells from replacing data in the Paste Area? No problem. Copy the cells then choose Edit, Paste Special. Check Skip blanks and hit OK.

Moving data within the same worksheet

Follow steps 1 thru 2 above but don't hold down Ctrl

Advanced copying

You can also use the Office Clipboard to copy and insert data – see page 24.

Excel 2003 allows you to be highly specific about which cell components are copied. You can use a special technique to limit the copy operation to specific aspects (but only one at a time); these include the cell format, underlying formulas, cell values, data validation rules or all cell contents and formats.

Performing specific copy operations

If you paste in copied (not moved) data via Ctrl+V or Shift+Insert, you can specify exactly what you want inserted. Just click the Insert Options button and make a choice in the menu.

1 Select a cell range

2 Hit Ctrl+C (or click here in the Standard toolbar)

	A	B	C
1	**Product/Service Catalog**		
2			
3	**Product/Service Name**	**Price**	
4	Fine Lamps	60	
5	Leather Chairs	85	
6	Hardwood Desks	175	
7			
8			
9			
10			
11			
12			
13			
14			
15			
16			
17			
18			

To copy/move only visible (not hidden) cells, first hit F5 then Special. Select Visible cells only. Now proceed as normal.

3 "Marching ants" define the area to be copied

4 Click the upper left cell in the Paste Area (the range you want to copy the data into)

Copying hidden data to Word (or any other app)? Only visible data makes it across.

5 Choose Edit, Paste Special

6 Select a component (e.g. Formulas or Validation) and/or an operation (e.g. Multiply or Divide). Optionally, click Transpose to change columns to rows (or vice versa). Finally, hit OK

External copy/move operations

You can easily copy or move a range of cells between worksheets and workbooks.

Moving data to another worksheet

You can merge cells (i.e. spread their content over more than one cell). Select a cell range then copy the data you want to merge into the top left cell. Hit this button:

in the Formatting toolbar then click OK.

To unmerge (split) the cell, click the button again (however, any surplus data discarded during the merge does not reappear).

1 Select a cell range

2 When the mouse pointer changes to an arrow, Alt+drag the range onto the relevant worksheet tab

| ◄◄ ◄ ► ►► \ Sheet1 / Sheet2 \ **Invoice** / |

3 Drag the cell range back into the worksheet area (the second worksheet is now displayed) and place it in the correct location

Copying data to another worksheet

Follow steps 1 thru 3 above but hold down Ctrl as well as Alt

Moving data to another workbook

1 Open both workbooks in separate windows and pre-select the target worksheet

To get the two workbooks in conveniently placed windows, choose Window, Arrange. Specify how you want the windows arranged (e.g. Tiled) and hit OK.

2 Select a cell range

3 When the pointer changes to an arrow, drag the range onto the relevant worksheet in the second workbook

Copying data to another workbook

Follow steps 1 thru 3 directly above but Ctrl+drag

Moving worksheets

To insert a new worksheet, click the tab (in the Tab area) which represents the sheet in front of which you want the new worksheet inserted. (To insert multiple sheets, hold down Ctrl and click the relevant number of tabs.) Finally, pull down the Insert menu and click Worksheet. (You can't undo this operation).

You rearrange the worksheet order within a given workbook. You can also transfer a worksheet to another workbook.

Rearranging worksheets

1 Click a single worksheet tab or Ctrl+click more than one

2 Drag the worksheet(s) to a new location in the Tab area

Moving worksheets to another workbook

1 Click a single worksheet tab or Ctrl+click more than one

2 Choose Edit, Move or Copy Sheet

To delete a worksheet, click its tab in the tab area. Pull down the Edit menu and click Delete Sheet. In the message which launches, click OK. (Deleting a sheet erases its contents, too!)

3 Click here; select the new host workbook from the drop-down list

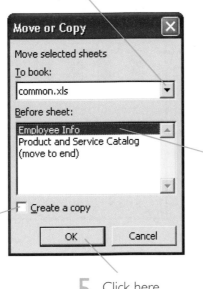

4 Click the worksheet in front of which you want the transferred sheet(s) to appear

Check this: to perform a copy operation rather than a move.

5 Click here

Copying data from Internet Explorer

A special relationship exists between Excel 2003 and Internet Explorer 5.x or later. You can use standard Windows techniques to copy data from Internet Explorer and paste it into Excel.

You can also drag-and-drop data from Internet Explorer into Excel.

Using drag-and-drop
With Excel 2003 and Internet Explorer both open in separate windows, do the following:

To select all data, press Ctrl+A.

Select the relevant data in Internet Explorer, then drag it into Excel 2003

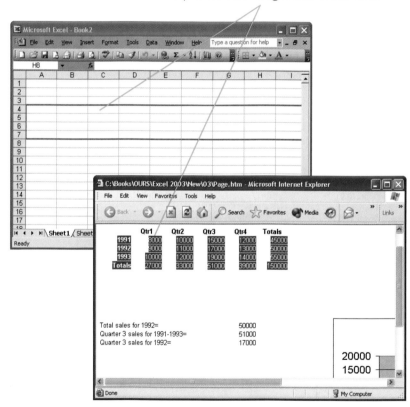

Workbook management

In Excel, workbooks are where it's at. Learn how to create new workbooks (blank or based on templates) in minutes then save and reopen them. You'll also convert your own workbooks into templates, to save time when you need to create new ones. Want to publish your workbooks on the Net? No problem – you'll soon be converting them to interactive or non-interactive HTML and XML and creating your own shared workspaces in real time. You'll also create "smart documents" that enhance template functionality and more prosaic workspaces that let you reload your working environment in a few mouse clicks.

Finally, you'll customize AutoRecover optimally, to make sure you can recover data in the event of loss.

Covers

Chapter Four

Creating new workbooks

Creating new workbooks is a cinch with templates. A template is a pre-designed workbook which is ready to use. The templates supplied with Excel 2003 contain numerous pre-defined fields, several pre-defined worksheets, preset formatting and special buttons which you can click to launch features directly.

As well as using the templates provided, you can create your own – see page 55. Alternatively you can create a new blank workbook and then customize it later – but hey, why take the long route?

Creating a workbook

If this incarnation of the Task Pane isn't onscreen, click the down-pointing arrow and select New Workbook.

1 Refer to the Task Pane on the right of the screen and do the following:

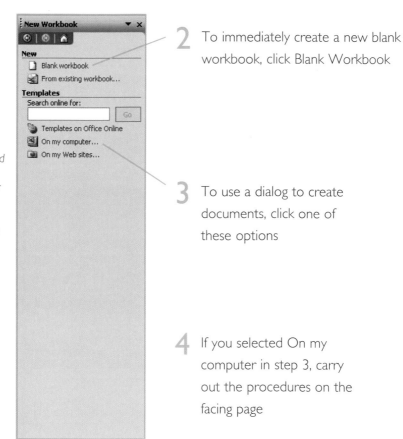

2 To immediately create a new blank workbook, click Blank Workbook

Hey, you selected "Templates on Office Online" or "On my Web sites" and can't see what to do? Please jump to page 54.

3 To use a dialog to create documents, click one of these options

4 If you selected On my computer in step 3, carry out the procedures on the facing page

5 Activate a tab

7 Preview the selected template

Templates you create are stored in the General tab – see page 55.

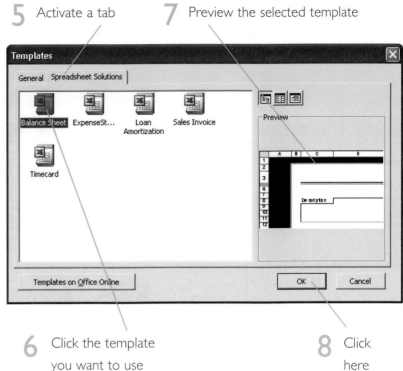

You can convert some workbook types – for example, templates – to "smart documents". These are programmed to provide assistance when you need it and make it even easier to share information by interacting with other programs like Word.

To make a workbook a smart document, you add a XML expansion pack. Choose Data, XML, XML Expansion Packs then hit Add. Locate and add the pack you need. (If Excel refuses to let you add a pack, consult your system administrator.)

6 Click the template you want to use

8 Click here

9 The new workbook launches

Intrigued and want to know more about smart documents? Go to: http://www.microsoft.com/office/editions/prodinfo/technologies/smartdocuments.mspx.

(If you're interested as a developer, try http://msdn.microsoft.com.)

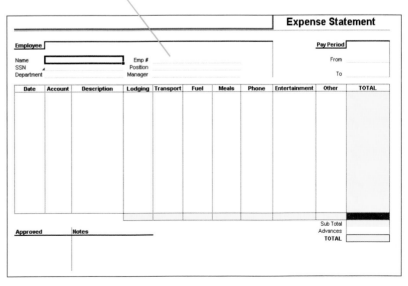

...cont'd

10 If you selected Templates on Office Online in step 3, use any of the templates on Office Online (for more on Office Online, see also pages 27 thru 28)

11 If you selected On my Web sites in step 3, use the dialog that launches to search for templates on your networked websites

Saving workbooks

You can save your files in XML format. XML is used to exchange data between dissimilar platforms and software. See page 62.

It's important to save your work at frequent intervals, to avoid data loss in the event of a hardware fault or power interruption.

Saving a document for the first time

1 Choose File, Save or File, Save As

2 Or hit Ctrl+S

You can enter as many commas and periods as you want in Excel names – for example, you could save a workbook as:
Results.04.provisional.xls.

4 Click here then select a drive/folder combination in the drop-down list. Or click any buttons on the left for access to the relevant folders

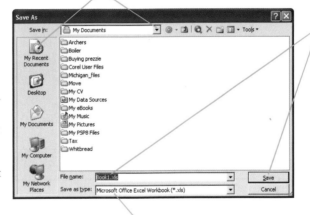

5 Type in a file name then click Save

Want to use your own extension in a save? Easy: just surround the name with quotes. For example, if you want to call a workbook **Results.03** *instead of* **Results.xls***, enter:* "Results.03".

3 Select a save format

Saving previously saved documents

1 Choose File, Save. Or hit Ctrl+S

Saving a workbook as a template

Basing new workbooks on templates saves a lot of time and effort.

By default, workbook templates appear as icons in the Templates dialog's General tab (page 53) and are saved to \Documents and Settings**user name**\Application Data\ Microsoft\Templates.

1 Want to have your template display a preview in the Templates dialog (page 53)? Choose File, Properties. Select the Summary tab and check Save preview picture

2 Perform steps 1–5 above but select Template (*.xlt) in step 3

Using Internet-based shortcuts

You can save workbooks – usually in HTML (HyperText Markup Language) or XML (Extensible Markup Language) format – to network, Web or FTP servers. You can do this so long as you've created a shortcut to the folder that contains them.

To create a shortcut to a Web/FTP folder, you must have a live Internet connection, rights to view/save files and its URL.

To create a shortcut to an intranet folder, you must have a network connection, rights to view/save files and its network address.

Creating shortcuts to FTP folders

1 Launch the Open or Save As dialog:

2 Select Add/Modify FTP Locations

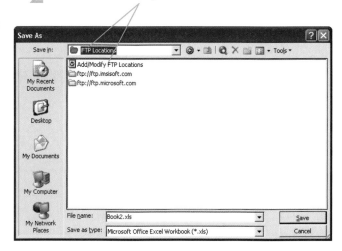

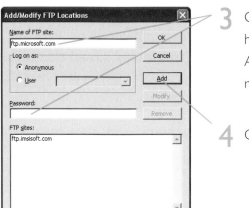

3 Complete the dialog (as here, some FTP sites are Anonymous and don't require a password)

4 Click Add

Creating shortcuts to Web folders

1 Launch the Open or Save As dialog:

3 Click here

Creating shortcuts to local network folders may require a different procedure. See your system administrator.

2 Click here

4 Complete the Add Network Place Wizard

Saving to Web/FTP shortcuts

1 Pull down the File menu and click Save As Web Page. Click in the Save as type: field and select Web Page (if it isn't already pre-selected)

2 Complete the rest of the dialog in the normal way then select a destination shortcut and a destination format. Click OK

Interactive v. non-interactive saving

You can combine interactive and non-interactive material in a single Web page. (You can also use data from other Office programs.)

This is a useful technique since it allows you to combine items which logically belong together. For example, you could create a page containing non-interactive data, an interactive chart, your logo and related text items...

You can save data to Web pages (on the Internet or intranets) in two ways: non-interactively and interactively. Both methods have one major advantage: it isn't necessary to have Excel 2003 in order to view the end result. You can save entire workbooks interactively or non-interactively, or just specific components. And you can use a mix-and-match approach: some parts of a saved workbook can be interactive (for example, salary details) while others (like logos and descriptive text) can likely be non-interactive.

Non-interactive saving

This is the method to use if you only want users to view, not interact with, your data. Users need only have access to the Internet or an intranet and an appropriate browser (e.g. Internet Explorer).

Saving non-interactively is also useful since you can "round-trip" the resulting HTML file between Internet Explore and Excel. When you do, most formatting and features can be brought back into Excel. Neat, huh?

You can edit Excel-produced HTML files directly from within Internet Explorer 5.x or higher. Click the Edit button in the toolbar.

Interactive saving

Interactively means that users viewing your data can also work with it in (basically) the same way that you do in Excel 2003. For instance, they can:

Items you can publish with interactivity include cell ranges, worksheets, Print Areas and charts. However, you may lose some formatting or features in the case of charts.

- rearrange cell ranges

- enter/update values

- calculate data

- implement sorts and filters

- reformat data

As with non-interactive saving, users can view interactive data in their browser, without needing to have installed Excel 2003. However, the interactive parts in the HTML file can't be opened and modified in Excel – no round-tripping. For this reason, when you publish interactively you should retain a master copy of the originating workbook. You can then amend this as required and republish it to the Web.

Preparing to save to the Web

There are several steps you should take before you begin any of the procedures on pages 60 thru 63:

1 Make sure your original Excel 2003 data is complete and correct (including the formatting)

2 Save the definitive version of your Excel workbook as a .XLS file, in the normal way, and keep this secure

3 Decide whether disseminating your data in standard .XLS format will be sufficient. This is an option if you happen to know that everyone who will view it has access to Excel 2003. If this is the case, jump to page 60 or 61, as appropriate. If it isn't, first carry out the remaining steps below

4 Decide whether you want to save to interactive or non-interactive Web pages (see the facing page)

5 It's a good idea – before you make your data available publicly – to save a test version of your Web page on your own PC. This means you can open it in your browser and confirm that everything is as it should be. If it isn't, you can re-export your data after you've made the necessary corrections within the original Excel 2003 file (see step 2)

Re step 6 – if you're publishing your data in standard .XLS format, carry out a different procedure: select Print Preview in Excel 2003's File menu to preview it. Press Esc when you've finished.

6 Preview the Web page (see page 60 for non-interactive previewing and step 9 on page 61 for interactive previewing)

7 Decide where you want to put the Web page

Non-interactive saving

Previewing your work before saving

Choose File, Print Preview

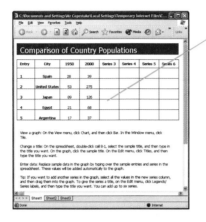

2 Your browser now launches, with your work displayed in it

Before you can save files to Web folders or FTP sites, you must first have set up the relevant shortcuts. See pages 56 thru 57.

Publishing an entire workbook non-interactively

Choose File, Save as Web Page

2 Click here. In the drop-down list, select a recipient/shortcut – see the pages 56 thru 57

Also follow steps 1 thru 3 if you've already selected the item you want to publish.

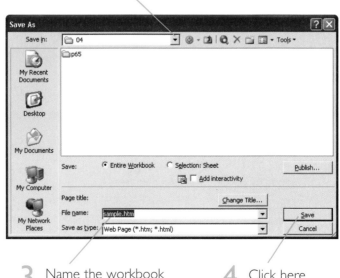

3 Name the workbook

4 Click here

Interactive or "mix-and-match" saving

To publish a workbook interactively, or to have some components interactive and others non-interactive, follow these procedures:

In the Viewing options section, make the appropriate selection in line with the following:

- *select Spreadsheet Functionality if you're exporting a spreadsheet or filtered list*
- *select PivotTable functionality if you're exporting a PivotTable*
- *select Chart functionality if you're exporting a chart (you must publish the chart separately from other worksheet contents – see also pages 175 thru 176)*

1 Choose File, Save as Web Page

2 In the Save As dialog, hit the Publish button

3 Select the type of data you want to publish

4 Optional – specify a data item

5 Optionally, check this for interactive saving

6 Click here

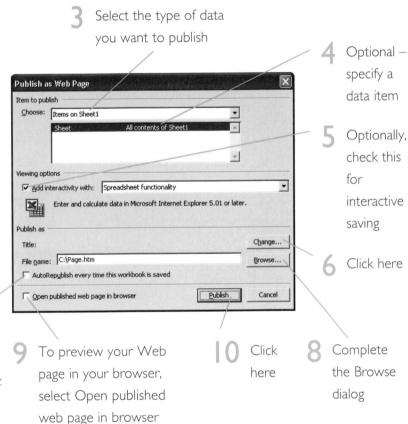

Check "AutoRepublish every time this workbook is saved" to have Excel automatically update your Web file each time you carry out a save operation. (Make sure you select the Refresh option in your browser when viewing.)

9 To preview your Web page in your browser, select Open published web page in browser

10 Click here

8 Complete the Browse dialog

To work with interactively saved data, browser users must have the following:

- *Internet Explorer 4.1 or later*
- *an appropriate Microsoft Office license*

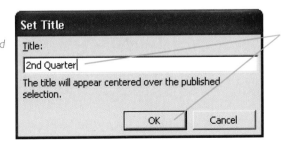

7 Name the published data then hit OK

Saving to XML

You can also publish Excel data on the Web in Extensible Markup Language (.XML) format, which focuses on describing/distributing data. Whereas HTML concentrates on describing how Web pages look, XML is the de facto language for data structuring and delivery on the Web. This is because it's platform-independent: it can be utilized across the Internet and specializes in exchanging data between dissimilar computers/platforms and software.

Saving to XML produces a specialized text file that conforms to specific guidelines and can be read by a wide variety of differing applications.

Saving to XML Spreadsheet format

Some formatting aspects are not retained when you export to XML Spreadsheet format. These include:

- *charts/chart sheets*
- *list functionality (though the underlying data remains)*
- *outlining*
- *custom views*

Additionally, to export password-protected worksheets and workbooks, you must first remove the password.

If you're using Office Professional Edition 2003 or the stand-alone version of Excel 2003, you have another option. You can export to XML data. Choose XML Data (*.xml) in step 3.

If this produces an error message, this likely is because you haven't yet added a XML map. Launch the XML Source Task Pane and click XML Maps. Select Add and locate the appropriate XML source file. The source now appears in the Task Pane; select elements then drag them onto the worksheet.

| Choose File, Save As

3 Click here then select a drive/folder combination in the drop-down list. Or click any buttons on the left for access to the relevant folders

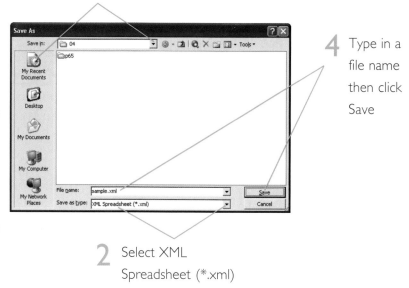

4 Type in a file name then click Save

2 Select XML Spreadsheet (*.xml)

Using AutoRecover

By default, Excel saves a recovery version of your work every 10 minutes. This, allied to Excel's Application Recover facility (page 23) is a very useful feature which helps to ensure that you don't lose data in the event of a crash or power failure.

However, you should not use AutoRecover as a substitute for saving your work in the normal way – regard it instead as a useful supplement in your data backup schedule.

Customizing AutoRecover

Pull down the Tools menu and click Options. Do the following:

You can turn AutoRecover off (though it's hard to imagine a good reason for doing so) by checking this:

Select the Save tab

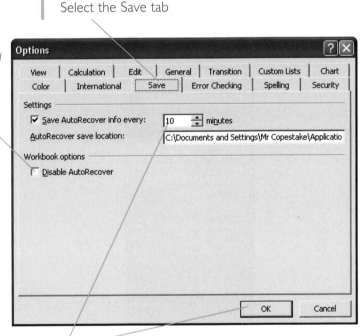

Excel lets you save your workbooks to a variety of third-party formats. To do this, carry out steps 1 thru 5 on page 55. In step 3, however, select an external format.

Want to close down all open workbooks in one go? Hold down one Shift key as you pull down the File menu and click Close All.

2 Type in a new AutoRecover interval (in minutes) then click OK

Opening workbooks

Excel 2003 uses some unusual techniques for opening workbooks.

1 Hit Ctrl+F1 if the Task Pane isn't onscreen

2 If your Task Pane is different, click the arrow and select Getting Started

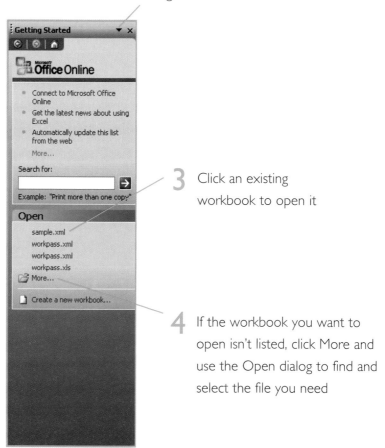

3 Click an existing workbook to open it

4 If the workbook you want to open isn't listed, click More and use the Open dialog to find and select the file you need

You can copy, rename or delete workbooks from within the Open dialog.

Right-click any workbook entry in the main part of the dialog. In the menu, click the desired option. Now carry out the appropriate action.

5 You can also launch the Open dialog directly: just press Ctrl+O

6 Want the Open dialog to default to a specific folder? Choose Tools, Options then select the General tab. In the Default file location field, type in the default folder. Finally, click OK

Opening Web/Intranet workbooks

From within Excel, you can open websites, Intranet sites or documents stored at FTP sites directly into your browser.

If the Web toolbar isn't currently onscreen, move the mouse pointer over any existing toolbar and right-click. In the menu which appears, click Web. Now do the following:

1 Ensure your Internet connection is live

2 Click Go

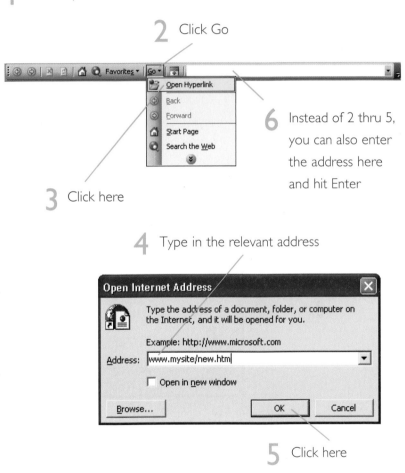

3 Click here

6 Instead of 2 thru 5, you can also enter the address here and hit Enter

4 Type in the relevant address

5 Click here

7 The site selected in step 4 is opened in your browser

Workspaces

Sometimes when you work with Excel 2003, you'll require more than one workbook open simultaneously or even just multiple worksheets open at the same time.

Instead of having to open each component separately, you can save details of your current working environment as a "workspace". When you've done this, you can simply reopen the workspace; Excel 2003 then opens the workbooks/worksheets for you.

Workspaces have a further application. You also can create shared workspaces as a great way of working with other people on workbooks in real time. These workspaces are Windows SharePoint sites.

Hit Ctrl+F1 then open the Shared Workspace Task Pane. Hit Create. If you encounter any problems from here on in, consult your site administrator.

Creating workspaces

1 Choose File, Save Workspace

2 Click here then select a drive/folder combination in the drop-down list. Or click any buttons on the left for access to the relevant folders

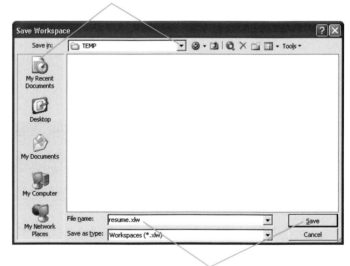

3 Type in a file name (the default is "resume.xlw") then hit Save

Opening workspaces

1 Hit Ctrl+O

2 Select Workspaces (*.xlw) in the Files of type field. Locate the workspace and click OK

Cell referencing

As you become more of an Excel guru, you'll need to define cell references in more than one way, according to the type of data you're working with. Mostly, you likely will use relative and absolute references but Excel also supports an older but easier-to-use system: R1C1. You'll also want to name cells and formulas because this makes them much more user-friendly. Luckily, there's a useful technique you can use to have Excel replace references in formulas with their equivalent names in just a few mouse clicks.

So far, you've only used the Range operator to create a cell range between two cell references. However, real Excel-savvy users need to make use of two further operators. Hey, what are you waiting for?

Covers

Chapter Five

Relative references

Excel 2003 lets you define cell references in various ways. Look at the next illustration:

	A	B	C	D	E
1					
2		**Product**	**Unit Price**	**Quantity**	**Amount due**
3		Widgets	$0.07	425	$29.75
4		Nuts	$0.13	246	
5		Bolts	$0.08	380	

The following formula has been inserted in cell E3:

C3*D3

This tells Excel to multiply the contents of C3 by D3. C3 and D3 are defined in relation to E3: C3 is in the same row (3) but two columns to the left (C), while D3 is in the same row but *one* column to the left. Excel calls this "relative referencing".

That these are relative references can be shown in the following way. If we use the techniques discussed on page 36 (AutoFill) to extend the formula in E3 to E4 and E5, this is the result:

C	D	E
Unit Price	**Quantity**	**Amount due**
$0.07	425	=C3*D3
$0.13	246	=C4*D4
$0.08	380	=C5*D5

Extrapolated cell references

Excel 2003 has extrapolated the references intelligently, correctly divining that the formula in E4 should be **C4*D4**, and that in E5 **C5*D5**.

Compare this process with the use of absolute (i.e. unchanging) references on the facing page.

Absolute references

Relative cell references can be very useful. However, there are situations when you need to refer to one or more cells in a way which *doesn't* vary according to circumstances.

Look at the next illustration:

	A	B	C	D	E	F
1	Interest rate =	6%				
2		**Product**	**Unit Price**	**Quantity**	**Amount due**	**Interest**
3		Widgets	$0.07	425	$29.75	$1.79
4		Nuts	$0.13	246	$31.98	
5		Bolts	$0.08	380	$30.40	

The reason the Interest rate is entered separately from the calculation is convenience: if the rate changes, it's much easier to update one entry rather than several.

Cell F3 contains a formula which multiplies E3 by B1. If this were inserted as:

=E3*B1

extrapolating the formula over F4 and F5 (with the technique we used on the facing page) would produce:

=E4*B2

and

=E5*B3

respectively.

Clearly, this is incorrect (in this instance) because the cell in which the Interest rate is entered doesn't vary. It's an absolute reference, and remains B1.

Entering absolute references

Entering an absolute reference is easy. Simply insert $ in front of each formula component which won't change.

So the correct version of the Interest formula in F3 would be:

=E3*B1

R1C1 referencing

A1 is the referencing method which Excel 2003 uses by default (and which has been used throughout this book).

Excel 2003 can also make use of an older, alternative style of referencing cells (called the "R1C1" method) that numbers both columns and rows. It has the advantage that the distinction between absolute and relative referencing is easier to understand. Its disadvantage is that it is not as brief as the A1 method.

Relative and absolute R1C1 referencing

In R1C1 style, Excel 2003 indicates absolute references in line with the following example:

R2C2   the equivalent of B2 in A1 style

You can also use mixed referencing. This uses an absolute column with a relative row or vice versa. With mixed referencing, when the location of a cell that contains a formula changes, Excel varies the relative component but not the absolute.

In other words, cell location is defined with an "R" followed by a row number and a "C" followed by a column number.

On the other hand, R1C1 relative references are enclosed in square brackets. Thus, if the active cell is B5, the relative cell reference **R[1]C[1]** refers to the cell one row down and one column to the right (i.e. C6).

Implementing R1C1 referencing

1 Choose Tools, Options

2 Activate the General tab

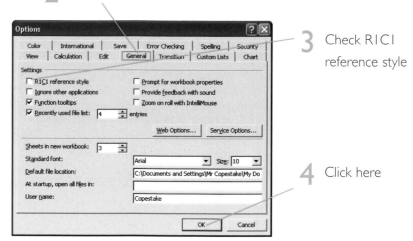

3 Check R1C1 reference style

4 Click here

Naming cells

An alternative way to reference cells is to give them a "name" or identifier which describes the contents. Naming cells is a much more user-friendly technique than working with cell coordinates.

Defining names with the Name box

The easiest way to define names for cells is to use the Name box on the Formula Bar.

| Select the cell(s) you want to name

2 Click here

Names (it doesn't matter if they're lower or upper case) may be up to 255 characters long. The following rules apply:

- *The 1st character must be a letter or underscore: _*

- *Other characters may be any sequence of letters, digits, underscores and full stops (but not spaces)*

- *Separators must be either an underscore or full stop i.e. to apply* **Interest Rate** *as a name, you could type in* **Interest_Rate**

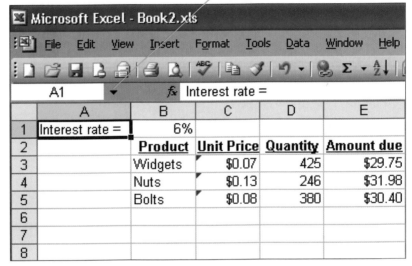

You can't use standard cell references (e.g. B2, H$12 and R3C4) as names.

3 Type in a name and press Enter

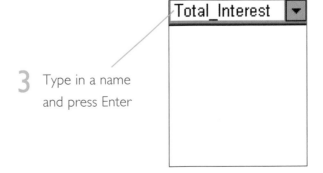

You can use the Go To dialog (F5) to locate named ranges: just select a name in the dialog and hit OK.

The Name box is an effective shortcut to applying and inserting names. However, you can also use a more comprehensive menu route to:

- define and apply new names

- apply existing names

- delete names

- substitute already defined names for cell references, either in selected cells or globally

- paste names into the Formula Bar

Defining/applying names – the menu route

To rename a name, select it. Type the new name and then hit Add. Finally, delete the old name by selecting it and then clicking Delete.

1 Select one or more cells

2 Pull down the Insert menu and choose Name, Define

3 Now carry out step 4 OR 5 below. Finally, perform step 6:

You can name formulas. In step 4, type in a name. In the Refers to box, type = followed by the formula. Click OK.

To use the named formula, press F2 in the relevant cell. Choose Insert, Name, Paste. In the Paste Name dialog, double-click the formula.

4 Type in a new name

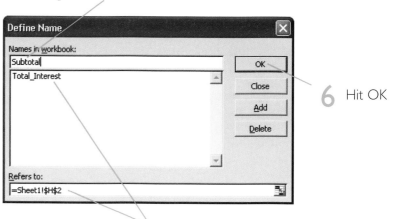

6 Hit OK

You can name cells in more than one worksheet. Follow step 4. Replace any reference in the Refers to field with =. Click the tab for the first worksheet you want to reference then Shift+click the last. Finally, select a cell or cell range.

5 Or click an existing name (you can also find out what it refers to by viewing its reference or formula in the Refers to field)

Substituting names in formulas

You can have Excel 2003 automatically replace normal cell references in formulas with the appropriate pre-defined names.

The illustration below should clarify the need for this:

C12	▼			f_x =SUM(E3:E5)		
	A	B	C	D	E	F
1	Interest rate =	6%				
2		**Product**	**Unit Price**	**Quantity**	**Amount due**	**Interest**
3		Widgets	$0.07	425	$29.75	$1.79
4		Nuts	$0.13	246	$31.98	
5		Bolts	$0.08	380	$30.40	
6						
7						
8						
9						
10						
11						
12		Total Amount Due	$92.13			
13						
14						

The example shown here is a particularly simple one; name substitution comes into its own in large worksheets.

C12 contains this formula:

=SUM(E3:E5)

If you want to limit the swap to a single cell, select it and one other which contains no formulas.

which totals E3, E4 and E5. If, however, these cells have had names allocated to them (e.g. Widget_total, Nut_total and Bolt_total), then it makes sense to adjust the formula in C12 accordingly. Fortunately, you can have Excel 2003 do this for you.

Substituting names for references
Do ONE of the following:

1 Select the cells which contain the formulas whose references you want converted to the relevant names

2 Click any one cell in the worksheet if you want *all* formula references converted to the relevant names

3 Choose Insert, Name, Apply

4 Click one or more names

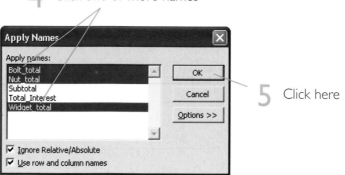

5 Click here

Excel 2003 lets you paste names directly into the Formula Bar while you're in the process of entering a formula. Select the cell into which you want to insert the formula. Activate the Formula Bar by clicking in it. Begin the formula by typing =. Now choose Insert, Paste. In the dialog, double-click a name.

The end result:

6 Excel 2003 has inserted the relevant names into the formula

You can "toggle" between reference types as you work with formulas. Click in the Formula bar, select a reference and press F4 repeatedly.

C12 f_x =SUM(Widget_total:Bolt_total)

	A	B	C	D	E
1	Interest rate =	6%			
2		**Product**	**Unit Price**	**Quantity**	**Amount due**
3		Widgets	$0.07	425	$29.75
4		Nuts	$0.13	246	$31.98
5		Bolts	$0.08	380	$30.40
6					
7					
8					
9					
10					
11					
12		Total Amount Due	$92.13		

Cell reference operators

We've already encountered one cell reference operator: the colon. This is known as the Range operator and is used to define the rectangular block of cells formed between the two cell references which it separates. For example, **B3:E5** defines the block of cells which begins with B3 and ends with E5.

However, there are two other reference operators. Look at the next illustration:

	A	B	C	D	E
1					
2		**Qtr1**	**Qtr2**	**Qtr3**	**Qtr4**
3	**2002**	8000	10000	15000	12000
4	**2003**	9000	11000	17000	13000
5	**2004**	10000	12000	19000	14000
6	**Totals**	27000	33000	51000	39000
7					
8	Quarter 3 sales for 2002 thru 2004 =				51000
9	Quarter 3 sales for 2003 =				17000

Reference operators have priority over all other operators – in other words, Excel actions them first.

Union operator

E8 contains this formula:

=SUM(D3,D4,D5)

The comma is known as the Union operator; it combines multiple references into one. In this case, the formula is totaling separate cells which could also be expressed as **D3:D5**. However, this need not be the case. For instance, it could show **B3,C5,E8**.

Intersection operator

E9 contains the following formula:

=SUM(B4:E4 D3:D5)

The space separating the two ranges is known as the Intersection operator. The formula returns the cell at the intersection of **B4:E4** and **D3:D5** – in other words, D4.

Problems

With Intersection operators, the defining ranges must overlap. If they don't, Excel 2003 returns an error message complete with a Smart Tag.

Click here

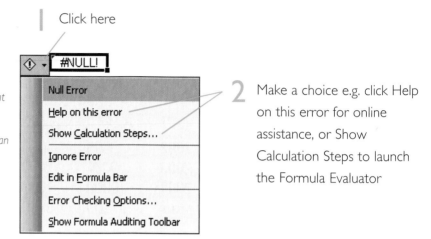

The first element in these Smart Tag menus is a statement, not an option.

2 Make a choice e.g. click Help on this error for online assistance, or Show Calculation Steps to launch the Formula Evaluator

Another common "problem" with Intersection operators is when Excel determines that there are cells with values next to the affected ranges. Excel assumes you may have wished to include some or all of these and produces another Smart Tag.

Click here

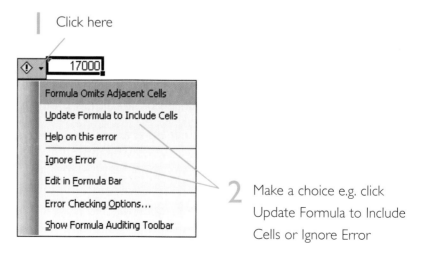

2 Make a choice e.g. click Update Formula to Include Cells or Ignore Error

Functions

Formulas get lonesome on their own – cheer them up by adding functions. Remember how you felt when your employers invited you to their Thanksgiving dinner? That's how good formulas feel when you insert functions: they make them work better, too. Excel 2003 has a large number of inbuilt functions which perform specialized calculations for wide-ranging applications e.g. statistical, math, financial etc. You'll learn how to use some of the most frequently used functions then top up your skills by using Office Online tutorials so, before you know it, you'll be a fully-fledged function black belt.

Covers

Chapter Six

Functions – an overview

Use the functions explored in pages 80 thru 86 of this chapter as examples (they'll give you a good idea of how to apply other functions) then take the Office Online tutorials on pages 87 thru 90.

Functions are pre-defined tools which accomplish specific tasks. These tasks are often calculations; occasionally, however, they're more generalized (e.g. some functions simply return dates and/or times). In effect, functions replace one or more formulas.

Excel provides a special dialog to help ensure that you enter functions correctly. This is useful for the following reasons:

- Excel 2003 provides so many functions, it's very convenient to apply (and amend) them from a centralized source: the Insert Function dialog

- the Insert Function dialog ensures the functions are entered with the correct syntax

Functions can only be used in formulas, and are always followed by bracketed arguments.

Recognizing functions

The following are examples of often-used functions:

You can use a shortcut (AutoCalculate or "AlwaysCalc", as Excel sometimes refers to it) to total a cell range. Select the range (but make sure all the cells aren't hidden – this produces an incorrect result). Refer to the right of the Status bar at the base of the screen; Excel displays the total in the format: **SUM=x** *(where "x" is the total).*

Ctrl+click any other cell to add this to the total.

AVERAGE	Finds the average of a range of numbers
COUNT	Counts cells containing numbers
COUNTA	Counts cells that aren't empty
IF	Verifies if a condition is true or false, and acts accordingly
LOOKUP	Compares a specified value with a specified cell range and returns a value
MAX	Finds the largest number in a range
MIN	Finds the smallest number in a range
PRODUCT	Multiplies numbers
SUM	Adds together a range of numbers

You can use other simple functions in AutoCalculate. Select a range then right-click over the Status bar total. Finally, select a function.

Some of these are explored later in the chapter.

Working with functions

Functions can only be used in formulas.

Inserting a function

Excel 2003 organizes its functions under convenient headings e.g. Financial, Date & Time or Statistical.

1 Just after you've typed = refer to the Formula bar and click this button: f_x

If you invoke this process after you've already typed in part of the formula, omit steps 2 thru 4.

2 Type in a brief description of the function you want and click here

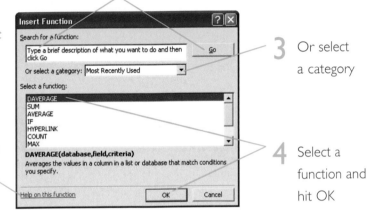

3 Or select a category

Want help with using a function? Click here:

4 Select a function and hit OK

5 Enter the function arguments

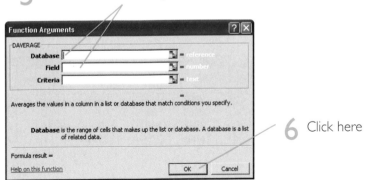

6 Click here

7 You can also type functions directly into a formula but only if you know the syntax. It's often easier to use the Insert Function dialog

The **SUM** function

The SUM function totals specified cells. You can insert a SUM function by using the Insert Function dialog – see page 79. However, you can also use a useful shortcut – AutoSum – to total adjacent cells automatically. Look at the next illustration:

You can use a shortcut here. Pre-select the cells you want to total before you carry out step 1. For instance, if you select B3:F6 and then click the AutoSum button, Excel 2003 inserts all relevant totals.

	A	B	C	D	E	F
1						
2		Qtr1	Qtr2	Qtr3	Qtr4	
3	2002	8000	10000	15000	12000	
4	2003	9000	11000	17000	13000	
5	2004	10000	12000	19000	14000	
6	Totals	27000	33000	51000	39000	

Click the arrow for access to additional AutoSum functions like Average and Count.

To total the range B3:E3 in F3, click cell F3

2 Click the AutoSum button in the Standard toolbar

3 Excel 2003 surrounds the cells it believes should be included in the SUM function with a dotted line

For more information on specific functions, hit F1. In the Assistance Task Pane, enter "common functions" in the Search for box and press Enter. In the list, click "Examples of commonly used formulas".

	A	B	C	D	E	F	G	H
1								
2		Qtr1	Qtr2	Qtr3	Qtr4			
3	2002	8000	10000	15000	12000	=SUM(A3:E3)		
4	2003	9000	11000	17000	13000	SUM(**number1**, [number2], ...)		
5	2004	10000	12000	19000	14000			
6	Totals	27000	33000	51000	39000			

4 If necessary, amend the formula entry in F3 then press Enter

5 Excel 2003 inserts the SUM function

The LOOKUP function

LOOKUP compares a value you set (the Look-Up value) with the first row or column in a Look-Up table. If it finds a matching value, it returns it in the cell you specify. If it doesn't, it returns the largest value in the table which is the same as or less than the Look-Up value. Alternatively, if the Look-Up value is smaller than all the values in the Look-Up table, LOOKUP returns an error:

LOOKUP can also work with text values or names.

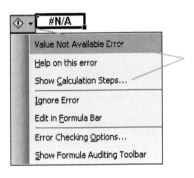

Click the Smart Tag and select an option e.g. Help on this error, or Show Calculation Steps to launch the Formula Evaluator

The values in the Look-Up table must be in ascending order. If they're not, you can rectify this.

Select the values. Pull down the Data menu and click Sort. In the Sort by section in the Sort dialog, make sure Ascending is selected. Finally, click OK.

Using LOOKUP

The Look-Up table   The Look-Up value

	A	B	C	D	E	F
1						
2						
3	Monthly lease rates per $1000 borrowed					
4	Years	Rates				
5	1	$22.50				
6	2	$26.58				
7	3	$47.31				
8	4	$49.22		Lease term in years=		50
9	5	$89.08		Lease value=		

Here, a Look-Up table and value have been established. In this instance, names have also been applied, for convenience:

- the table (B5:B9) is Lease_Table

- the value (F8) is Lease_Term

To enter the LOOKUP function, follow steps 1 thru 8 on page 82.

1 Select the relevant cell (in the example on page 81, F9)

2 Follow step 1 on page 79

3 Follow step 2 on page 79 but type in "lookup" (no quotes)

4 Follow step 4 on page 79 but select LOOKUP

5 Double-click
lookup_value,array

Re step 6 – in this example, names have been entered since they've been applied to the relevant cells.

6 Enter function arguments. In Lookup_value, type "Lease_Term"; in Array, type "Lease_Table" (omit the quotes). Click OK

7 The inserted formula

	F9	▼	f_x =LOOKUP(Lease_Term,Lease_Table)			
	A	B	C	D	E	F
1						
2						
3	Monthly lease rates per $1000 borrowed					
4	**Years**	**Rates**				
5	1	$22.50				
6	2	$26.58				
7	3	$47.31				
8	4	$49.22			Lease term in years=	50
9	5	$89.08			Lease value=	$49.22
10						
11						

8 LOOKUP has returned the highest value under 50

The IF function

The IF function checks whether a specified condition is TRUE or FALSE and carries out one or more specified actions accordingly.

Look at the next illustration:

An advanced tip – you can "nest" IF functions within themselves (up to a total of 7 times) by using brackets within brackets. For more help with this, hit F1. In the Assistance Task Pane, enter "IF function" in the Search for box and press Enter. In the list, select IF worksheet function. See Example 3 in the HELP text.

	A	B	C	D
1				
2				
3		**Name**	**Amount Spent**	**Discount**
4				
5		Brierley	$1,280	
6		Jones	$1,020	
7		Mitchell	$570	
8		Harrison	$1,150	
9		Wood	$870	
10				
11				

Here, individual customer discounts need to be calculated in D5:D9. Each discount in D5:D9 depends on these conditions:

- if the amount a customer has spent is greater than or equal to $1000 then the discount is 20%

- if the amount a customer has spent is less than $1000 then the discount is 10%

Using the IF Function

1 Select the cell you want to host the function – in the case of the example above, D5 (initially)

2 Follow step 1 on page 79

3 Follow steps 2 and 4 on page 79. In step 2, type in "logical test" (omit the quotes); in step 4, select IF

4 Enter the "Logical test", "Value if true" and "Value if false" arguments – see below

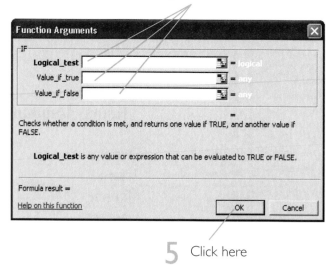

5 Click here

Arguments

Logical test	The condition. In this instance: C5>=1000 (i.e. the contents of C5 must be greater than or equal to 1000)
Value if true	The action to be taken if the condition is met. In this instance: C5*20% (i.e. the contents of C5 are multiplied by 20%)
Value if false	The action to be taken if the condition isn't met. In this instance: C5*10% (i.e. the contents of C5 are multiplied by 10%)

The IF function uses comparison operators.

Name	Amount Spent	Discount
Brierley	$1,280	256
Jones	$1,020	204
Mitchell	$570	57
Harrison	$1,150	230
Wood	$870	87

6 The IF function has been inserted into D5 then the cells below with AutoFill

The **HYPERLINK** function

You can use the HYPERLINK function to insert links to documents on network servers, intranets/the Internet and local hard disks.

Hyperlinks can also include pointers to:

You can also insert hyperlinks via a more conventional method.

Right-click the text or picture you want to serve as a hyperlink. In the menu, click Hyperlink. On the left of the Insert Hyperlink dialog, select a hyperlink type (e.g. Existing File or Web Page). On the right, select a file/ worksheet, or type in a Web/ email address, as appropriate. Click OK.

- specific cells or ranges in Excel 2003 worksheets

- Word 2003 bookmarks

Using the **HYPERLINK** function

1 Select the cell you want to host the function

2 Follow step 1 on page 79

3 Type in "hyperlink" (no quotes) and click Go

4 Click HYPERLINK
    then OK

...cont'd

5 Enter the hyperlink address

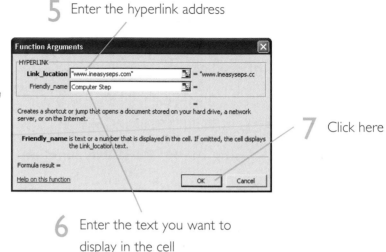

7 Click here

6 Enter the text you want to display in the cell

8 To activate the hyperlink, click it (this links to Computer Step's website)

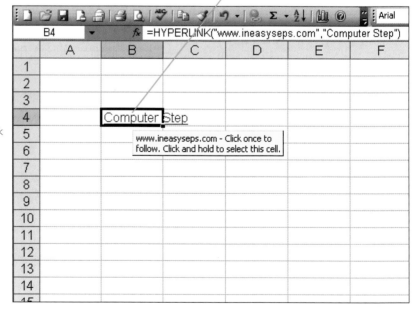

Online help with functions

Okay, so functions are a tad complex, especially when you get into math or statistical functions. Excel does its best to make them easy to use – the Insert Function dialog takes you thru each stage – but hey, there's no harm in getting some extra help, right?

Right, that's why those nice folks at Office Online have provided some peachy-keen tutorials you can use to master functions.

Help with functions generally

1 Type this into your browser's Address Bar then hit Enter:

http://office.microsoft.com/training/training.aspx?AssetID=
RC061914861033&CTT=4&Origin=CR061831141033

2 Read the Overview then hit
Next to work thru the tutorial

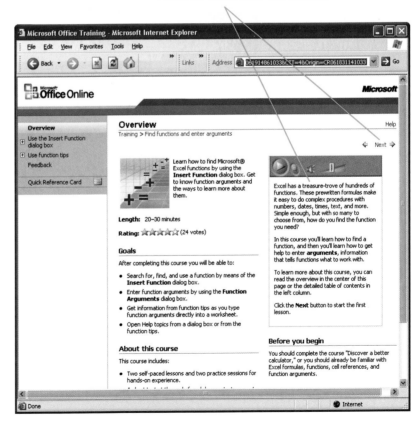

Help with time-based functions

This tutorial uses a fun approach but still shows you how to create a timecard.

1 Type this into your browser's Address Bar then hit Enter:

http://office.microsoft.com/training/training.aspx?AssetID=
RC060796661033&CTT=4&Origin=CR061831141033

2 Read the Overview then hit
Next to work thru the tutorial

3 This is a more advanced course, so only take it if you're
reasonably up on functions

Help with date-based functions

This tutorial shows you how to calculate with dates and – like the others – incorporates a short (unscored) test.

1 Type this into your browser's Address Bar then hit Enter:

http://office.microsoft.com/training/training.aspx?AssetID=
RC061771061033&CTT=4&Origin=CR061831141033

2 Read the Overview then hit
Next to work thru the tutorial

3 Again, only run this tutorial when you've made progress with basic functions

Help with statistical functions

This tutorial uses a fun approach but still shows you how to create a timecard.

Many of Excel 2003's statistical functions (like CONFIDENCE, GROWTH, INTERCEPT, TREND, VAR and VARA) have been enhanced, especially their rounding results. They also operate with increased precision.

So don't be surprised if the statistical function you use returns a different result than it would have in previous versions of Excel: it should be considerably more accurate.

1 Type this into your browser's Address Bar then hit Enter:

http://office.microsoft.com/training/training.aspx?AssetID=
RC010919231033&CTT=4&Origin=CR061831141033

2 Read the Overview then hit
Next to work thru the tutorial

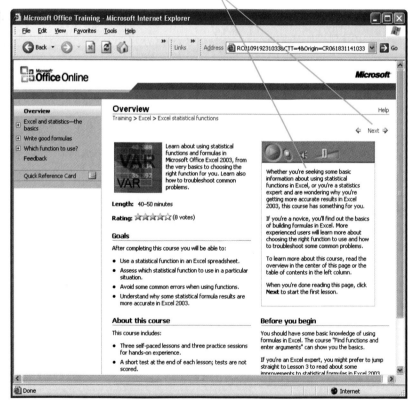

3 Run the course on page 87 before trying this one

Cell errors and auditing

Given the eventual size of most worksheets, problems sometimes occur when Excel 2003 is unable to evaluate a formula. Error messages appear when this happens – here, you'll learn how to deal with them. Messages are shown "on-the-fly", with reference to specific examples and also with the appropriate corrections.

Excel 2003 supplies a comprehensive set of auditing tools. You'll learn how to use these to track dependent and precedent cells and to trace errors, so you can feel confident about creating and troubleshooting your own formulas. You'll also use a dialog route to pinpoint cells which are in conflict with formulas and discover a new way to launch the Watch Window.

Finally, you'll insert comments into cells, and edit or delete them subsequently.

Covers

Chapter Seven

Cell errors

The error messages on this and subsequent pages are accompanied by Smart Tags whose associated menus list the error type and provides various related options. Perhaps the most useful is Show Calculation Steps. Select this to launch the Formula Evaluator and use this to step through each stage of the suspect calculation.

The following table shows details of some of the common Excel error messages (they're shown in action in the illustration below).

#DIV/0!   In this instance, this error is caused by an attempt to divide 2.5 by zero. Theoretically this should generate infinity. In practice any such value is too big, even for a computer, and the calculation is suppressed. (Sometimes, Excel treats blank cells in formulas as zeros)

#N/A   This means that No value is Available. The LOOKUP argument (B8, B5:D6) should refer to cell D8 instead of B8; B8 – since it contains text – is incorrect

#NAME?   Excel 2003 fails to recognize the name of the function "IS", which has been incorrectly typed for "IF". In general, make sure you haven't mistyped names

#NULL!   This formula uses the intersection operator (a space) to locate the cell at the intersection of ranges B15:D15 and A16:A18. Since they don't intersect, Excel 2003 displays the error message

	Data/error messages			Formulas which caused the errors

	A	B	C	D	D
1	(1)				
2		2.5	0	#DIV/0!	=B2/C2
3					
4	(2)				
5	Amount:	$0	$500	$1,000	1000
6	Discount:	0.0%	5.0%	10.0%	0.1
7					
8		Price =		$750	750
9		Discount Rate =		#N/A	=LOOKUP(B8, B5:D6)
10					
11	(3)				
12		-0.25		#NAME?	=IS(B12=0, "Zero", "Non-zero")
13					
14	(4)				
15		5	10	15	15
16	2				
17	4				
18	6			#NULL!	=B15:D15 A16:A18

Here are some additional error messages and details of their causes:

#NUM!   This error value indicates problems with numbers. The first example of this error (see below) attempts to generate the value 100^{1000}, i.e. 100 multiplied by itself 1000 times. This is too large for the computer to store and so the calculation is suppressed. This error often occurs with iterating functions. In this case, adjust Excel's iteration rate; choose Tools, Options, select the Calculation tab, check Iteration then adjust the max. value upwards

In the second example the attempt to calculate the square root (SQRT function) of a negative value is suppressed

The number of hash symbols varies according to the size of the host column.

#VALUE!   This error occurs when the data in a cell isn't appropriate for the operation, or the operation doesn't apply to the type of data. Here an attempt has been made to divide "Text" by 50

This error is not necessarily generated by a formula. In this case the number stored is simply too long for the cell width. Another possible cause is a negative date or time

Data/error messages

	A	B	C	D
20	(5)			
21		100	1000	#NUM!
22		16		#NUM!
23				
24	(6)			
25		Text	50	#VALUE!
26				
27	(7)			
28				########
29				
30	(8)			
31		100		
32			50	2

Formulas which caused the errors

D
=B21^C21
=SQRT(-B22)
=B25/C25
100000000
=B31/C32

The final error message we'll discuss here is more complex:

The examples on pages 92 thru 94 are simple, practical illustrations of the causes of error messages. In practice, tracking down the origin of an error message is sometimes less than straightforward, because a single error may cause a proliferation of error values.

(See pages 95 thru 99 for tracking techniques.)

#REF!   To generate this error requires another stage. On page 93, the formula in D32:

=B31/C32

divides the contents of cell B31 by the contents of cell C32, initially producing the correct answer. However, if Excel can't locate one of the cells referred to (e.g. if B31 no longer exists because row 31 has been deleted), it displays this message

This process is demonstrated in the illustration below:

#REF! only appears if you've deleted the cell referred to by a formula; clearing the cell's contents (e.g. by selecting it and clicking Clear, Contents in the Edit menu) will, instead, produce "0".

2   The formula has changed; the B31 component has been replaced by #REF! and C32 has now become C31

	A	B	C	D	E	F	G
				D31 ▼			
20							
21		100	1000	#NUM!			
22		16		#NUM!			
23							
24							
25		Text	50	#VALUE!			
26							
27							
28				########			
29							
30							
31				ⓘ ▼ #REF!			
32							

Cell reference: D31 ƒ =#REF!/C31

Menu items shown:
- Invalid Cell Reference Error
- Help on this error
- Show Calculation Steps...
- Ignore Error
- Edit in Formula Bar
- Error Checking Options...
- Show Formula Auditing Toolbar

Since row 31 has been deleted and the reference in the formula to B31 is invalid, Excel 2003 displays the error message (complete with Smart Tag)

Auditing tools

Auditing displays tracer arrows between cells. In order to make these arrows more visible, you may wish to hide worksheet gridlines.

Pull down the Tools menu and click Options. Activate the View tab; in the Window options section, deselect Gridlines. Finally, click OK.

Excel 2003 provides a variety of features you can use to ensure formulas work correctly. You can use the Formula Auditing toolbar to have Excel delineate cell relationships with arrows ("tracers"). In this way, if a formula returns an error message, you can (literally) track down which cell is misbehaving.

Cells which are referred to by a formula in another cell are called precedents. For example, if cell H26 has the formula:

=M97

M97 is a precedent.

Inserting precedent tracers

1 Choose Tools, Options. Activate the View tab; in the Objects section, ensure Show all is selected then click OK

2 Click the cell whose precedents you want to display

3 Choose Tools, Formula Auditing, Show Formula Auditing Toolbar

Tracer arrows vanish if you change the formula they point to, insert rows/columns or delete/move cells. To reinstate them, repeat step 4.

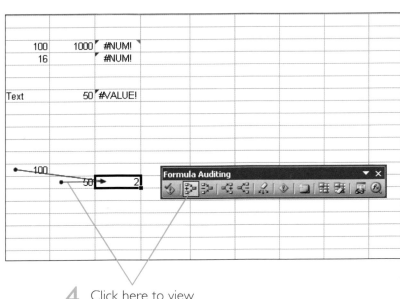

4 Click here to view precedent tracers

Cells which contain formulas referring to other cells are called dependents. For instance, if cell H6 has the formula:

=SUM(C6:D8)

H6 is a dependent cell (and the cells in the range C6:D8 are precedent cells).

Inserting dependent tracers

1 Choose Tools, Options. Activate the View tab; in the Objects section, ensure Show all is selected then click OK

2 Click the cell whose dependents you want to display

3 If the Formula Auditing toolbar isn't currently onscreen, choose Tools, Formula Auditing, Show Formula Auditing Toolbar

Double-click any arrow to select the cell at the other end. However, if the cell is in another worksheet or workbook, double-click the black arrow then a reference in the list that appears.

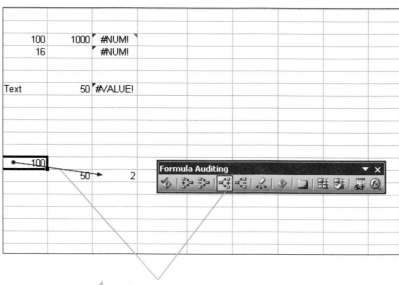

4 Click here to view dependent tracers

Using the Error Tracer

When a formula returns an error, you can use another auditing tool – the Error Tracer – to track it back to its source and correct it.

Some items can't be traced. These include text boxes, charts (except those on a separate chart sheet) and formulas in other workbooks (if they aren't currently open).

Using the Error Tracer

1 Click the cell which contains an.error value

2 Choose Tools, Options. Activate the View tab; in the Objects section, ensure Show all is selected

3 If the Formula Auditing toolbar isn't currently onscreen, choose Tools, Formula Auditing, Show Formula Auditing Toolbar

Since tracer arrows disappear if you carry out certain actions, it's a good idea to print out the worksheet with the arrows, for reference.

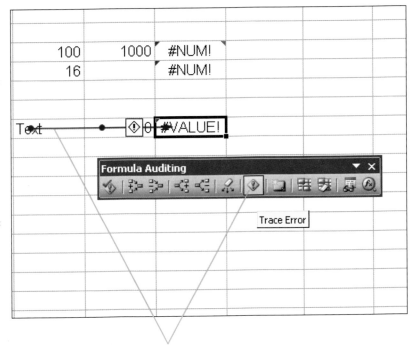

If Excel beeps when you carry out a trace, it has either found all the relevant levels or you're trying to trace the wrong type of item.

4 Click here to delineate the error

Clear existing tracer arrows (step 1 page 99) before reusing the Error Tracer.

5 The Error Tracer locates all cells affected by the error. So, if the error has multiple incorrect paths, Excel will only flag the first path. Repeat step 4

Checking validated cells

Cells that you've validated prevent the entry of data that is outside the permitted criteria. However, there are situations in which invalid data can still be inserted. For example, if a validated cell contains a formula/function that pulls in data from other cells, the result can contravene the validation.

Luckily, you can flag validated cells that contain invalid content.

1 Choose Tools, Options. Activate the View tab; in the Objects section, ensure Show all is selected

2 If the Formula Auditing toolbar isn't currently onscreen, choose Tools, Formula Auditing, Show Formula Auditing Toolbar

3 C9 contains the formula **=SUM(B3:C3)** but will only accept values within the range 100 thru 110

Entering valid data into the invalidated cell will also remove the circle.

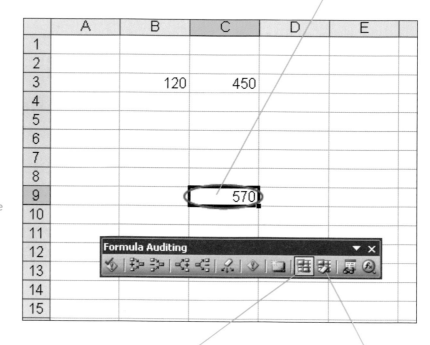

4 Click here to circle invalidated cells

5 This button removes the circle

More on the Formula Auditing toolbar

The Formula Auditing toolbar is really useful when it comes to tracking down errors. We've already looked at some of its applications but there are others. The illustration below gives you more information.

Use the Watch Window to inspect misbehaving formulas.

I To remove all tracer arrows (for instance, when you've finished the audit or perhaps to start again from a different cell), click here

5 Click here to insert a new comment (see also overleaf)

2 You can use a special dialog to facilitate error checking. Click this button then follow step 3

4 Click here to launch the Watch Window

3 Click Help on this error (for assistance), Show Calculation Steps (to launch the Formula Evaluator) or Edit in Formula Bar (followed by Resume when you're done) to correct the formula in the worksheet

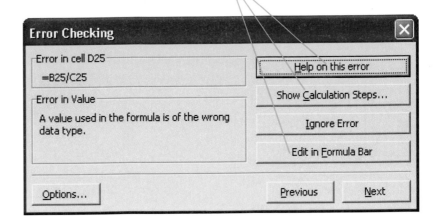

Working with comments

If the Comment flag doesn't appear, choose Tools, Options then Click the View tab. Select Comment indicator only.

You can attach comments to cells. Once inserted, comments can be viewed or edited whenever you want.

1. Select a cell

To have all comments (and flags) display all the time, choose Tools, Options. Activate the View tab. Select Comment & indicator. Click OK.

2. Choose Insert, Comment or carry out step 5 on page 99

3. Type in the comment then click outside the box

To print comments, choose File, Page Setup. Select the Sheet tab then an option in the Comments box.

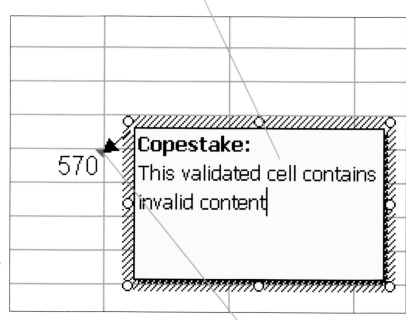

> 570
>
> **Copestake:**
> This validated cell contains invalid content

Comments appear truncated? Choose Window, Unfreeze Panes. Or enlarge the comment box (see step 6).

4. Cells that contain a comment have a red flag – move the mouse pointer over this to launch and edit the comment

5. To move a comment, click its border then drag it to a new location

To work thru comments in sequence, choose View, Comments. Then use these buttons in the Reviewing toolbar to step thru each comment:

6. To resize a comment, click its border then drag a handle

7. To delete a comment, right-click the flag then select Delete Comment

Workbook security

Nowadays, with widespread Internet and intranet use, data security is a real hot potato. However, Microsoft has thought of this and Excel 2003 has comprehensive security features.

First, you'll "protect" cells, a technique which allows you to specify precisely which cells can and can't be amended. Then you'll protect specific cell ranges and specify precise details of which operations can be carried out, and by who. You'll also prevent unauthorized users from modifying workbook structure and resizing windows, and use Information Rights Management to restrict access to sensitive data.

Finally, you'll allocate passwords to workbooks then reopen them and (if necessary) change the passwords. Just make sure you don't lose the passwords.

Covers

Chapter Eight

Protecting cells

Most of the mechanisms discussed in this chapter will not make data secure against determined attempts to access it. Instead, look on them as techniques to:

- *hide data that might be confusing to some users*
- *prevent other users from accidentally altering your data*

If a file contains confidential information, keep it in a secure place with restricted access.

Individual cells can be protected so that they can't be amended, resized, deleted or moved. This is a two-stage process:

1. "Unlocking" those cells which you'll want to amend *after* the host worksheet has been protected (you won't be able to modify any of the other cells)

2. Protecting the worksheet

Unlocking cells

1 Select the cells you want to unlock

2 Hit Ctrl+I

If you check Hidden, any formulas in the cells will be hidden (if you've protected the worksheet) and won't appear in the Formula bar.

4 Uncheck Locked   3 Select the Protection tab

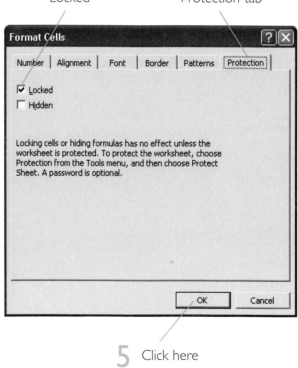

5 Click here

In summary, Excel 2003 lets you protect your data on various levels:

- *you can protect entire workbooks from being viewed and amended*
- *you can protect cell ranges*
- *(to a lesser extent) you can protect specific cells*

You can also enhance your protection strategy with Information Rights Management (page 107).

6 Alternatively, to unlock cells for specific users, complete the Allow Users to Edit Ranges dialog (page 104)

…cont'd

To modify cell protection, choose Tools, Protection, Unprotect Sheet. If necessary, type in the relevant password and click OK. Then select the relevant cells. Press Ctrl+1. Activate the Protection tab and select or deselect Locked, as appropriate. Click OK. Finally, perform steps 1–4 again.

Protecting the host worksheet

1 Pull down the tools menu and select Protection, Protect Sheet

2 Check this

3 Optional – enter a password (used if you want to unprotect the sheet – see the HOT TIP)

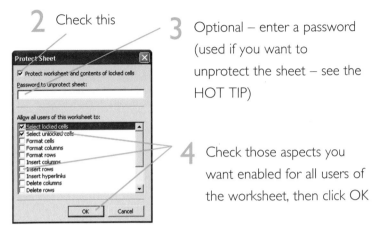

4 Check those aspects you want enabled for all users of the worksheet, then click OK

Running a macro which attempts to carry out a protected operation sends it to the Great Compiler in the Sky.

The effects of cell protection

When you've protected cells, the following results apply:

1. Any attempt to overwrite or edit a locked cell produces a special message:

You can have Excel warn you when you're about to open a workbook containing macros (see Chapter 15) that might contain viruses. However, Excel can't actually verify whether viruses are present; it can only warn you of the possibility…
Choose Tools, Macro, Security. Activate the Security Level tab. Select a protection level. (If this operation fails, see your network administrator.)

2. When a locked cell is selected, certain menu commands are grayed out

3. If any cell (locked or unlocked) is selected, pressing Tab will move the cursor to the next locked cell (the movement is from top to bottom, and left to right). Pressing Shift+Tab reverses the direction

Protecting cell ranges

You can protect specific ranges within worksheets.

Setting up range protection

Select a range then click the Permissions button to specify which users can amend these cells. In the Permissions dialog, hit the Add button and enter users (for help with the syntax, hit the "examples" link).

1 Pull down the Tools menu and click Protection, Allow Users to Edit Ranges

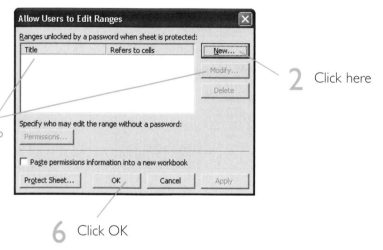

2 Click here

Select a range then hit Modify to change the users that are allowed to edit it.

6 Click OK

3 Name and specify a range (prefix it with = in the Refers to cells box)

Keep a list of passwords (and which workbooks they apply to) in a safe place.

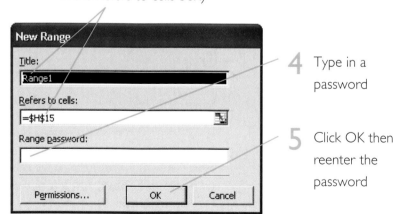

4 Type in a password

5 Click OK then reenter the password

7 Follow steps 1 thru 4 on page 103

Protecting workbooks

You can "protect" two workbook aspects.

Structure
This prevents users from:

- viewing hidden worksheets

- manipulating worksheet names

- inserting new worksheets or chart sheets

- copying/moving worksheets to another workbook

- recording macros

Windows
This prevents users from resizing or repositioning windows (although you can still hide/unhide them).

Protecting an entire workbook
Pull down the Tools menu and do the following:

To remove protection from the active workbook, pull down the Tools menu and click Protection, Unprotect Workbook. If necessary, type in the relevant password. Click OK.

Want to hide an entire workbook? No problem: simply choose Window, Hide. To get it back, hit Window, Unhide then double-click it in the Unhide dialog box.

You can protect shared workbooks, but if you want password-protection you'll have to apply it before you share the workbook.

1 Choose Tools, Protection, Protect Workbook

2 Check either or both of these

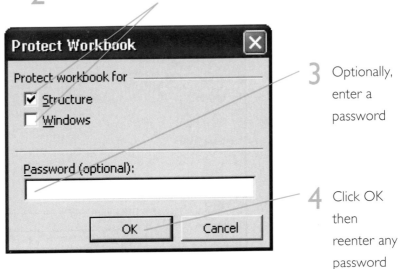

3 Optionally, enter a password

4 Click OK then reenter any password

Password-protecting workbooks

These passwords are in addition to the protection afforded by the Protect Workbook dialog box (page 105).

You can protect your workbooks by:

- allocating an "Open" password

- allocating a "Modify" password

The first allows users to open the associated workbook but prevents them from saving changes under the existing filename. The second allows users to modify and save the workbook.

Passwords are case-sensitive and can contain up to 255 characters – more than you'll need. They can be any combination of letters, numbers, spaces and other symbols.

Allocating a password

*You should give serious thought to the password you choose. For example, all passwords should consist of an easily memorable combination of upper- and lower-case letters, symbols, spaces and numerals. **P89aL $43X** would be an effective password (if you could recall it) while **Opensesame8** definitely wouldn't.*

1   Choose File, Save As

2   In the Save As dialog box, select where you want to save the workbook, allocate a name etc. (see page 55)

3   Click here

Lose or forget the password and you won't be able to recover the workbook!

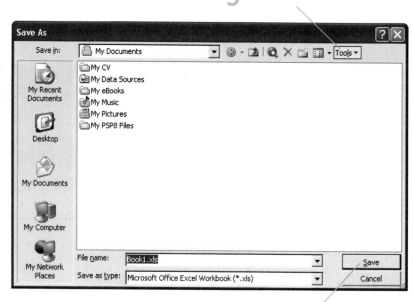

10   Proceed with the save

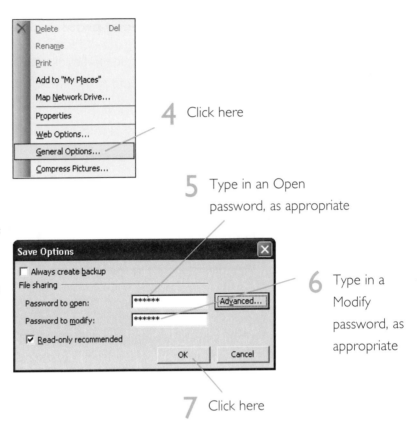

4 Click here

As a way of controlling sensitive information, you can use a new feature called Information Rights Management to restrict access to sensitive workbooks (but only if you're using Microsoft Office Professional Edition 2003 or the standalone version of Excel 2003). You do this via the Permission dialog box – File, Permission, Do Not Distribute.

You may have to download and install the Windows Rights Management client before you can proceed.

5 Type in an Open password, as appropriate

6 Type in a Modify password, as appropriate

7 Click here

8 Reiterate the Open password and click OK

Want to know more about Information Rights Management? Point your browser at this Office Online site: *http://office.microsoft.com/ assistance/preview.aspx? AssetID=HA010397891033.*

There is also a free trial IRM service. For more information, go to: *http://office.microsoft.com/ assistance/preview.aspx? AssetID=HA010721681033& CTT=98.*

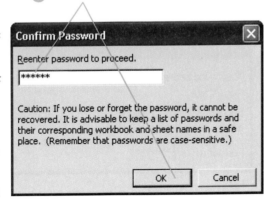

9 Reiterate your Modify password, if you entered one, and hit OK

Opening protected workbooks

 Once passwords have been allocated to a file, you can modify or remove them.

With the file open, pull down the File menu and click Save As. Carry out the procedures on pages 106 thru 107 to allocate one or more new passwords. (To remove passwords, leave their fields blank.)

Opening a password-protected workbook

1 Open the protected workbook (see page 64)

2 If you allocated an Open password, enter it here

3 Click here

If the workbook you're opening has had a Modify password allocated to it, Excel launches a further dialog.

 If you enter the wrong Open or Modify password, Excel 2003 launches a message. Click OK. Now repeat the relevant procedures. When you reenter the password(s), however, ensure that:

• the Caps Lock key is not active

• you type in the password with the correct capitalization (passwords are case-sensitive)

4 To open the workbook with the ability to modify it and save changes under the original name, type in the Modify password and carry out step 5

5 Click OK

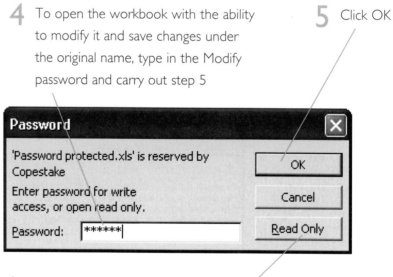

6 Or click Read Only to open the workbook as a "read-only" file (any amendments you make must be saved under a new name).

Data analysis

Data changes all the time and so you oftentimes will want to analyze it and look for trends. Luckily, predicting the effects of varying data is one of Excel's strong-points.

In this chapter, you'll explore how to preview changes to selected data values without necessarily implementing them. This sort of "what-if" process is something Excel is really good at. You'll also make speculative predictions based on current figures and formulas. Data tables can get pretty big and so it's useful to switch to manual (rather than automatic) calculation. Finally, you'll reformulate data dynamically (just by dragging fields) with PivotTables and PivotCharts.

Covers

Chapter Nine

Data analysis – an overview

Look at the following worksheet extract:

Excel recalculates formulas in dependent cells when the values in precedent cells are changed. If the network of dependent formulas is large, you may have to wait for the update to finish. This is frustrating if you wish to change several values and have to wait after each one while the rest of the worksheet is recalculated. See the tips below for work-arounds.

To turn on manual calculation globally, pull down the Tools menu and click Options. In the Options dialog, activate the Calculation tab. Select Manual in the Calculation section and hit OK.

To invoke manual calculation within all open worksheets, simply press F9. To invoke manual calculation within the active worksheet only, press Shift+F9.

	A	B	C	D
1				
2		**Video Rentals**		
3				
4		Rental Price=		$2.00
5		Number of Rentals=		250
6		Total Income=		$500
7				
8		Total Costs=		$200
9				
10		Net Profit=		$300

D6 contains the formula D4*D5 and D10 contains D6-D8. You'll encounter these formulas later in this chapter

Here, we have a simple worksheet which calculates the Net Profit based on several data values relating to the renting out of videos.

You should bear the following in mind:

Total Income (D6) = Rental Price (D4) x Number of Rentals (D5)

Net Profit (D10) = Total Income (D6) – Total Costs (D8)

The formulas contained in the extract are detailed in step 1.

Later topics in this chapter will explore various techniques which let you interpolate data into the extract. Changes to data values will ripple through the extract automatically and can be viewed at will and later discarded, if required.

Using Goal Seek

Refer to the illustration on the facing page and consider the following:

Let's suppose we need to know the number of video rentals necessary to break even. In other words, we want to find out how many rentals are necessary to meet the total costs, thereby ensuring that the net profit is $0. In the case of a simple example like this, you could arrive at the correct figure manually, by trial and error, without too much time and effort and without being a math guru. However, more complex worksheets would clearly make this approach much too time-consuming to be practicable.

Instead, however, you can use a Goal Seek What-If test. This sounds like a mouthful but this technique is easy once you get the hang of it.

Applying a Goal Seek What-If test

1   Select the cell that contains the formula you want to resolve

2   Choose Tools, Goal Seek

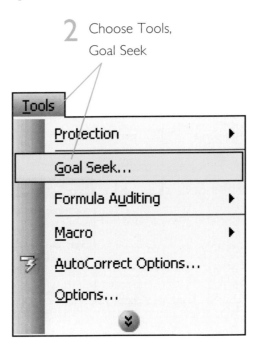

3 Type in the target value (in this case, 0)

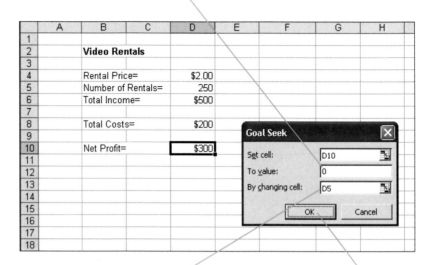

4 Type in the reference of the cell you want to change (in this case, D5)

5 Click here

6 Excel 2003 has calculated the What-If value...

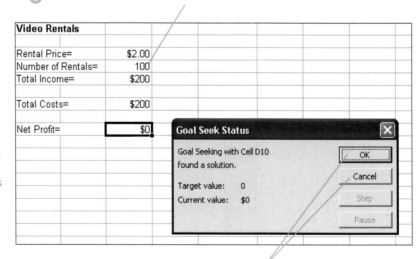

The ability not to implement the Goal Seek results makes this a useful technique for exploring alternatives.

7 Click OK to update the worksheet or Cancel to return to the original values

One-variable data tables

Irrespective of whether data tables have changed, they automatically recalculate when you recalculate the host worksheet.

You can, however, speed the process up. Pull down the Tools menu and click Options. In the Options dialog, select the Calculation tab. Check Automatic except tables. Click OK.

Please refer back to the illustration on page 110 and consider the following additional question:

Let's suppose we wanted to know how the Net Profit would change when the Rental Price is changed. We could do this using the simple What-If technique of varying the Rental Price and recording the corresponding change in the Net Profit. However, it would be necessary to repeat this for as many separate rental price values as we wished to test.

There's a much simpler and quicker route: you can use a one-variable data table.

Applying a one-variable data table

Re step 2 – if you insert values in a column, the formula cell must be in the row above the first value and one cell to the right. If you type in values in a row, though, it must be in the column to the left of the first value and one cell below.

One-variable tables will only work if these conditions are met.

2 Type in the formula which returns the Net Profit (here, you simply refer to the cell so just type: =D10)

	A	B	C	D	E	F	G	H
1								
2		**Video Rentals**				**Rental Price**	**Net Profit**	
3							$300.00	
4		Rental Price=		$2.00		$1.00		
5		Number of Rentals=		250		$1.25		
6		Total Income=		$500		$1.50		
7						$1.75		
8		Total Costs=		$200		$2.00		
9						$2.25		
10		Net Profit=		$300		$2.50		
11								
12								
13								
14								
15								
16								
17								
18								

1 In a row or column (in this case, F4:F10), type in the values for which you want to generate alternatives

You must select both *columns* or *rows* (but not the headings).

3 Select the table then choose Data, Table

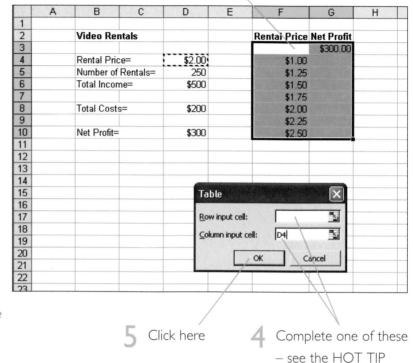

Re step 3 – complete the Column input cell field if you created a columnar table, the Row input cell field if you created a row-based table.

You should enter the reference of the input cell for which the initial table values (in this case, F4:F10) are to be substituted. Here, enter "D4" (no quotes).

5 Click here

4 Complete one of these – see the HOT TIP

Rental Price	Net Profit
	$300.00
$1.00	$50.00
$1.25	$112.50
$1.50	$175.00
$1.75	$237.50
$2.00	$300.00
$2.25	$362.50
$2.50	$425.00

6 The completed one-variable table

Two-variable data tables

Refer to the illustration on page 110 and consider the following:

So far, the examples we've examined have been fairly simple. Suppose, however, that we need to know how the Net Profit would vary relative to the Rental Price AND the Number of Rentals . . . Excel 2003 has a technique we can use to extrapolate this, too, despite the increased complexity of the operation. We need to use a two-variable data table.

Applying a two-variable data table

1 Construct the appropriate table – refer to the illustration below as a guide

2 Select the cell at the intersection of the row containing the first input values and the column containing the second – here, F4

	B	C	D	E	F	G	H	I	J	K
1										
2	**Video Rentals**				**Rental**			**Net Profit**		
3					**Price**			**Number of Rentals**		
4	Rental Price=		$2.00		$300.00	100	125	150	175	200
5	Number of Rentals=		250		$1.00					
6	Total Income=		$500		$1.25					
7					$1.50					
8	Total Costs=		$200		$1.75					
9					$2.00					
10	Net Profit=		$300		$2.25					
11					$2.50					
12										
13										
14										
15										
16										
17										
18										
19										
20										
21										

3 Press F2 and type in the formula which relates to the two input categories. In this example, the input categories are "Rental Price" and "Number of Rentals". Therefore, the cell which relates to them is D10 (i.e. "Net Profit") and the formula is: =D10

4 Select the table – the selection must include:

- the formula cell (F4 in the example on page 115)
- the row and column of input data (F5:F11 and G4:K4 in the example on page 115)
- the empty body of the table (G5:K11 in the example on page 115)

5 Choose Data, Table

6 Type in the reference for the cell which relates to the number of rentals i.e. D5

Make sure you've entered formulas in this table correctly – if you haven't, the two-variable data table won't function properly.

	B	C	D	E	F	G	H	I	J	K
1										
2	Video Rentals				Rental			Net Profit		
3					Price		Number of Rentals			
4	Rental Price=		$2.00		$300.00	100	125	150	175	200
5	Number of Rentals=		250		$1.00					
6	Total Income=		$500		$1.25					
7					$1.50					
8	Total Costs=		$200		$1.75					
9					$2.00					
10	Net Profit=		$300		$2.25					
11					$2.50					

Table

Row input cell: D5

Column input cell: D4

OK   Cancel

8 Click here

7 Type in the reference of the cell which relates to the rental price i.e. D4

The table shows at a glance the rental price/ number of rentals relationship.

Rental			Net Profit		
Price			Number of Rentals		
$300.00	100	125	150	175	200
$1.00	-$100.00	-$75.00	-$50.00	-$25.00	$0.00
$1.25	-$75.00	-$43.75	-$12.50	$18.75	$50.00
$1.50	-$50.00	-$12.50	$25.00	$62.50	$100.00
$1.75	-$25.00	$18.75	$62.50	$106.25	$150.00
$2.00	$0.00	$50.00	$100.00	$150.00	$200.00
$2.25	$25.00	$81.25	$137.50	$193.75	$250.00
$2.50	$50.00	$112.50	$175.00	$237.50	$300.00

9 The completed table

What-If scenarios

Refer back to the illustration on page 110 and consider this:

Let's suppose we need to forecast the effect of changing the following values:

- the Rental Price (D4)

- the Number of Rentals (D5)

- the Total Costs (D8)

You can create scenario summary reports. Click the Summary button in the Scenario Manager dialog. Follow the onscreen instructions.

We could simply input revised values into the worksheet and observe the effect. However, if the revisions are simply speculative, or if we need to input them more than once (or in varying combinations), it's best to use a scenario.

A scenario is simply a set of values you use to forecast the outcome of a worksheet model. You can:

To amend values in an existing scenario, select it in the Scenario Manager dialog. Click the Edit button. Now complete the Edit Scenario and Scenario Values dialogs in line with steps 3 thru 8 overleaf. Finally, perform step 9.

- create new scenarios

- switch to and view existing scenarios

- return to the original worksheet values via Undo (Ctrl+Z)

Creating a What-If scenario

1 Choose Tools, Scenarios

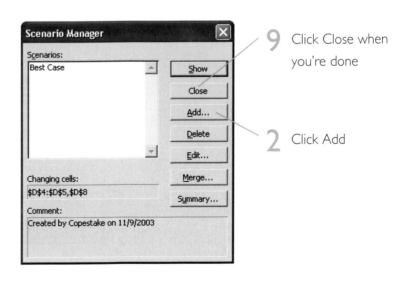

9 Click Close when you're done

2 Click Add

3 Name the scenario

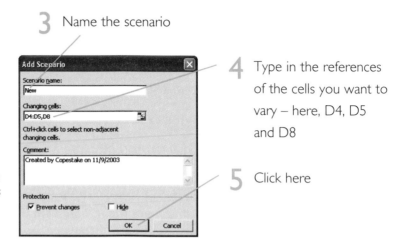

4 Type in the references of the cells you want to vary – here, D4, D5 and D8

5 Click here

To prevent anyone else amending your scenario, ensure Prevent changes is checked.
To hide it in the Scenario Manager dialog, check Hide.

6 Type in What-if values (overwrite the original figures)

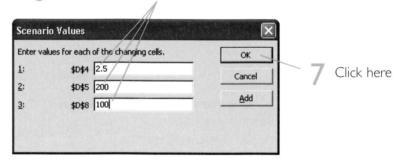

7 Click here

You can merge scenarios from different worksheets or workbooks. Choose Tools, Scenarios. Hit the Merge button then select a workbook/worksheet.

8 To view the scenario's effect, click Show in the Scenario Manager – notice that the changes have also cascaded into the two-variable data table

	B	C	D	E	F	G	H	I	J	K
1										
2	**Video Rentals**				**Rental**		**Net Profit**			
3					**Price**		**Number of Rentals**			
4	Rental Price=		$2.50		$400.00	100	125	150	175	200
5	Number of Rentals=		200		$1.00	$0.00	$25.00	$50.00	$75.00	$100.00
6	Total Income=		$500		$1.25	$25.00	$56.25	$87.50	$118.75	$150.00
7					$1.50	$50.00	$87.50	$125.00	$162.50	$200.00
8	Total Costs=		$100		$1.75	$75.00	$118.75	$162.50	$206.25	$250.00
9					$2.00	$100.00	$150.00	$200.00	$250.00	$300.00
10	Net Profit=		$400		$2.25	$125.00	$181.25	$237.50	$293.75	$350.00
11					$2.50	$150.00	$212.50	$275.00	$337.50	$400.00
12										
13										

PivotTables

You can also use external data sources (you may be prompted to install Microsoft Query). Click the relevant option and then complete the subsequent dialog boxes.

Another technique for reformulating information in a different way is the use of PivotTables. PivotTables provide much greater precision than any of the methods discussed earlier, and they function dynamically.

Using PivotTables

1 Click in the list or select the relevant range. Pull down the Data menu and click PivotTable and PivotChart Report

2 In the first dialog of the PivotTable and PivotChart Wizard, select "Microsoft Excel list or database". Ensure "PivotTable" is selected, then click Next

Re step 4 – click New worksheet or Existing worksheet. In the case of the second, enter the reference of the cell which will form the upper-left corner of the PivotTable.

3 In the second dialog, click Next

4 In the third and final dialog, select where you want the PivotTable created. Click Finish

5 Drag any of the fields in the PivotTable Field List window to the appropriate PivotTable section...

PivotTables are particularly useful when you need to compare totals relating to detailed lists of figures. You can use PivotTable interactivity to resummarize data very conveniently.

Click this to refresh your PivotTable data.

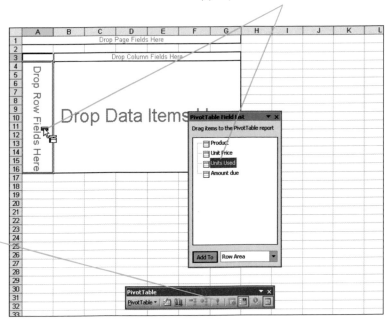

...cont'd

PivotTables are dynamic: you can drag any of the existing fields to new locations – or add new ones from the PivotTable Field List window – and Excel updates the PivotTable accordingly.

6 The new PivotTable

	A	B	C	D	E
1	Drop Page Fields Here				
2					
3	Sum of Amount due	Unit Price ▼			
4	Units Used ▼	$0.07	$0.08	$0.13	Grand Total
5	246			31.98	31.98
6	380		30.4		30.4
7	425	29.75			29.75
8	Grand Total	29.75	30.4	31.98	92.13

If you find PivotTables difficult, you'll be glad to know that Office Online offers some useful tutorials. Start at: http://office.microsoft.com/ training/training.aspx? AssetID=RC010136191033&CTT= 1&Origin=EC010229861033& QueryID=kfO4vYpg10.

Two of the fields in the list shown on page 122 – "Units Used" and "Unit Price" – have been associated with "Amount Due".

Using PivotTable AutoFormat

You can reformat PivotTables by applying AutoFormats (combinations of formatting characteristics). You can choose from more than 20.

1 Click in the PivotTable

2 Choose Format, AutoFormat

3 Click an AutoFormat

You can create interactive charts linked to PivotTable data. Click a cell in the PivotTable. Choose Insert, Chart. The new PivotChart is dynamic: you can add new fields or reposition existing ones just by dragging.

For a normal, non-interactive chart, copy PivotTable data. Select a blank cell and choose Edit, Paste Special. Select Values and hit OK. Now choose Insert, Chart and complete the wizard.

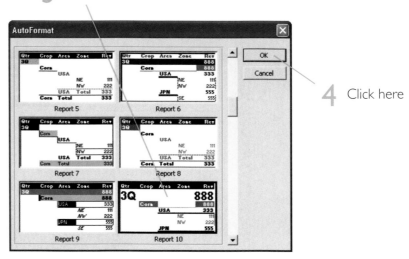

4 Click here

Using lists

One of the great things about worksheets is that you can also use them to store data in lists. Lists are sort of like mini databases. There are restrictions on the amount of data they can contain but these are so large you likely will not exceed them. Excel 2003 lets you manage lists so that they return the data you want to view at any given time. You can also create XML and SharePoint lists.

First you'll learn how to create lists in just a few seconds, then you'll sort them in various ways to make your data more accessible. You can also filter data, so that information you don't want to view is temporarily excluded.

Covers

Chapter Ten

Creating a list

- *use only 1 list per worksheet*
- *the first row in any list must label the columns*
- *ensure rows have similar values in each column*
- *make sure column names are formatted differently from data in the list*
- *ensure the list is surrounded by at least 1 blank row AND 1 blank column*
- *don't insert blank rows or columns within the list*
- *don't use spaces at the start or end of list cells*

You can hide the borders of inactive lists: choose Data, List, Hide Border of Inactive Lists.

You can't create lists in shared or protected workbooks.

There are limits to the number of columns lists can have but don't worry: they vary from 16 (date/time fields) to 64 (text and hyperlink fields).

In Excel 2003, a list is a series of worksheet rows that contain associated data. Excel now regards lists as quite distinct from other data: they function as databases. When they do:

- the list columns become fields

- the column labels act as field names

- each row in the list is a unique record

1 Select the cell range you want to convert into a list (it can already contain data or it can be blank)

2 Hit Ctrl+L

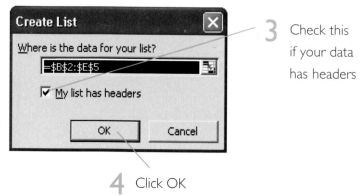

3 Check this if your data has headers

4 Click OK

5 The completed list is surrounded by a blue border

Product ▾	Unit Pric ▾	Units Use ▾	Amount du ▾
Electricity	$0.07	425	$29.75
Gas	$0.13	246	$31.98
Water	$0.08	380	$30.40
*			

6 Enter or amend data in the usual way

...cont'd

Click in the list to make it active.

Resize the list by dragging on the bottom right-hand corner (but first make sure no total row is displayed).

Inserting a new row/record

Produc ▼	Unit Pric ▼	Units Use ▼	Amount du ▼
Electricity	$0.07	425	$29.75
Gas	$0.13	246	$31.98
Water	$0.08	380	$30.40
*			

When the list is active, the blue asterisk denotes an insert row; type in (or paste) the new row

If you copy and paste data into lists, you may have to reimpose the original data type (Ctrl+1).

Displaying a total row

If the List toolbar isn't onscreen, choose View, Toolbars, List

You can create XML lists too. Open the XML Source Task Pane and drag elements onto the worksheet.

2 Click here

Produc ▼	Unit Pric ▼	Units Use ▼	Amount du ▼
Electricity	$0.07	425	$29.75
Gas	$0.13	246	$31.98
Water	$0.08	380	$30.40
Fuel	$1.56	245	$382.20
*			
Total			$474.33 ▼

None
Average
Count
Count Nums
Max
Min
Sum
StdDev
Var

If you publish lists on SharePoint sites, try these work-arounds if you encounter problems:

- *apply shorter names to lists*
- *see your site administrator – he/she may have denied access to the site or there may be a conflict between Excel and the site*

3 Excel inserts the total

4 Optionally, click here and select a new function

List operations

Filtering lists

You can display only those list/database rows (records) which contain specific data.

1 | In the column you want to filter, click the AutoFilter arrow

When columns have had AutoFilter applied to them, the arrow in the box turns blue.

Produc ▾	Unit Pric ▾	Units Use ▾	Amount du ▾
Electricity	$0.07	425	$29.75
Gas	$0.13	246	$31.98
Water	$0.08	380	$30.40
Fuel	$1.56	245	$382.20
✳			

To revert a list to normal cells, click in the list then choose Data, List, Convert to Range.

2 | Click the value you want to display

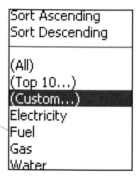

```
Sort Ascending
Sort Descending

(All)
(Top 10...)
(Custom...)
Electricity
Fuel
Gas
Water
```

In ascending sorts, Excel sorts in a specific order (shown first to last):

- numbers (minus to positive)
- alphanumeric (left to right and character by character)
- logical values (FALSE precedes TRUE)
- error values
- blank cells

The order is reversed for descending sorts (except that blank cells are still last).

3 | To create more complex filters, select Custom above. Specify an operator then a value it must match. Optionally, select And or Or then choose a second criterion. Hit OK

4 | To remove AutoFilters, pull down the Data menu and click Filter, AutoFilter

Basic list sorts

| Follow steps 1 thru 2. However, in step 2 select Sort Ascending or Sort Descending

Advanced list sorting

To sort rows by 2 or 3 columns, perform steps 5 thru 7 (in 5, select Sort top to bottom). Carry out steps 3 thru 4; repeat them in respect of the "Then by" fields, as appropriate. Follow step 8.

To sort by 4 columns, click a cell in the list and choose Data, Sort. In the Sort by box, select the least important column and click OK. Relaunch the Sort dialog. Select the most important column in the Sort by field, and the other two columns – in order of importance – in the Then by fields. Click OK.

To use a data form to add a new record (row) to a list, click in the list. Choose Data, Form. In the form, click New. Enter data for the new record then hit Enter. Repeat for as many records as you want to add. Finally, click Close.

When numbers are wrongly formatted as text in lists, Excel sorts detect this and treat the "text" as numbers.

1 Click any cell in the list

2 Choose Data, Sort then:

- to perform a simple sort in ascending or descending order, carry out steps 3 thru 4
- to sort list columns based on row contents, perform steps 5 thru 7 first, then follow steps 3 thru 4 (also complete the "Then by" fields lower down the dialog, as appropriate)

3 Click here; select the column you want to sort by

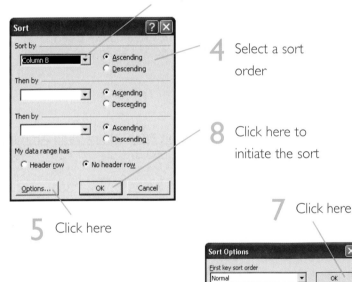

4 Select a sort order

8 Click here to initiate the sort

5 Click here

7 Click here

6 Select Sort left to right (this sorts by rows – Sort top to bottom sorts by columns)

Applying criteria

The example used here is an instance of one condition applied over more than one column. You can also use several conditions in one column.

AutoFilter filters are relatively limited: the only comparison operator you can use is =. Enter criteria.

Applying criteria

1 Ensure your worksheet has a minimum of three blank rows (the "criteria range") over the data you want to filter

2 In the data, copy the column labels which relate to the values you want to specify as filters

In the criteria range on the right, all of the following criteria must be true for rows to display:

- *the "Product" must be "Gas"*
- *the "Unit Price" must be greater than "$0.09"*
- *fewer than 400 units must have been used*

3 Paste the labels into the first blank row of your criteria range

4 Type in the criteria immediately below the criteria labels

Product	Unit Price	Units Used	
Gas	>0.09	<400	
Product	**Unit Price**	**Units Used**	**Amount due**
Electricity	$0.07	425	$29.75
Gas	$0.13	246	$31.98
Water	$0.08	380	$30.40

5 Click anywhere in the data then choose Data, Filter, Advanced Filter

To apply the filter in a different location, click here then – in the Copy to field – type in the reference of the cell you want to form the upper-left corner of where you want the filtered rows inserted.

6 Type in the criteria range reference (plus the labels)

8 To remove a filter, choose Data, Show All

7 Click here

Multiple worksheets/workbooks

Gotten lots of worksheet windows and not sure what to do with them? In this chapter, you'll learn how to rearrange them to best effect. You'll also set up data links between worksheets and workbooks – this is an important way to avoid data overload. You'll learn more about 3D references in formulas then discover how to achieve a useful overview by hiding rows and columns. An even better way to view data selectively is to apply manual and automatic outlining (together with styles).

Finally, you'll split worksheets into separate panes (so each can be viewed separately), freeze them for independent scrolling and compare workbooks side-by-side.

Covers

Chapter Eleven

Viewing several worksheets

OK, this isn't exactly a high-tech solution but it is a great way to beat a common Excel problem: worksheets becoming so large that it's hard to view the data you need.

Excel 2003 also lets you view multiple worksheets simultaneously. This can be particularly useful when they have data in common. Viewing multiple worksheets is a two stage process.

To open a new window, pull down the Window menu and click New Window

To switch between active windows, pull down the Window menu and click the relevant entry in the list at the bottom. Or hit Ctrl+F6.

Excel tells you you're working with an alternative view by incrementing a number in its title in the menu bar. For example, the worksheet "new" will have "new:1", "new:2" and so on.

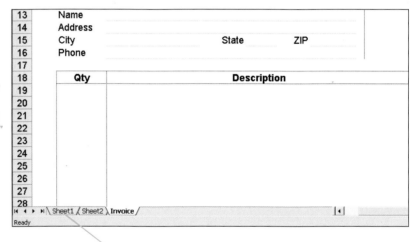

If you want to work with alternative views of the same worksheet – a useful technique in itself – simply omit steps 2–3.

2 Excel now launches a new window showing an alternative view of the active worksheet. Click the relevant sheet tab

3 Repeat step 2 for each new sheet you want to view

4 For best effect, refine the way the windows are arranged – see the facing page

Rearranging worksheet windows

When you have multiple worksheet windows open at once, you can have Excel arrange them in specific patterns. This is useful because it makes worksheets more visible and accessible. Options are:

Tiled — Windows are displayed side by side:

Horizontal — Windows are displayed in a tiled column, with horizontal subdivisions:

Vertical — Windows are displayed in a tiled row, with vertical subdivisions:

Cascade — Windows are overlaid (with a slight offset):

Rearranging windows

Pull down the Window menu and click Arrange. Then:

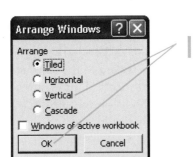

Click an arrangement then select OK

Links within a single workbook

Excel sometimes calls workbook links "external references", and links to other programs "remote references".

Consider the following examples:

	A	B	C	D	E
1		**Sales Figures 2003**			
2		Qtr1	Qtr2	Qtr3	Qtr4
3		$9,000.00	$11,000.00	$17,000.00	$13,000.00

	A	B	C	D	E
1		**Sales Figures 2004**			
2		Qtr1	Qtr2	Qtr3	Qtr4
3		$10,000.00	$12,000.00	$19,000.00	$14,000.00

Here, we have extracts from two separate worksheets within the same workbook. The first records sales figures for 2003, the second sales figures for 2004. In the excerpts shown, the amount of data is small; there is really no reason why both sets of data shouldn't have been recorded on a single worksheet. However, where you're concerned with large amounts of data, it *is* a very good idea to record them on separate worksheets. By the same token, if you needed to record and collate the totals it would be advantageous to do this on a third worksheet…

In a link, if the name of another worksheet or workbook has characters which aren't alphabetic, you must enclose the name or path in single quotes.

Using lots of smaller worksheets (as opposed to a single, much larger sheet) produces the following benefits:

- your worksheets will recalculate faster (because large worksheets are much more unwieldy)

- it's much easier to remain in control of your worksheets

- you can create different views of your data by setting up a report workbook that contains links to only some of the data

To remove the prompt from automatic updating, choose Tools, Options. Select the Edit tab. Uncheck Ask to update automatic links. Click OK. Now links are updated automatically at file startup, with no user involvement.

When you do use separate worksheets, you can "link" the relevant data. To revert to the earlier example, the totals in the third worksheet could be linked to the relevant data in the 2003 Sales and 2004 Sales worksheets. This ensures that, when the contents of any of the relevant cells on the subsidiary worksheets are changed, the totals are automatically updated.

...cont'd

When you create a link, the "source" file holds the original information while the "destination" file shows a copy of the data (because it retains only the address of the source file). As a result, the source file must always be accessible.

When you amend the source file while the destination file is active, the link in the destination file is updated automatically.

Updating also occurs:

- *(the usual method) every time you open the destination file – you choose whether to update*

- *when you perform a manual update. Choose Edit, Links. In the Edit Links dialog, select the relevant link(s) and click Update Values. Click OK*

Use the Edit Links dialog to housekeep links. You can break them (Break Link), open the source file (Open Source), change to a new source file (Change Source) and check whether a link has been updated (Check Status).

Establishing links

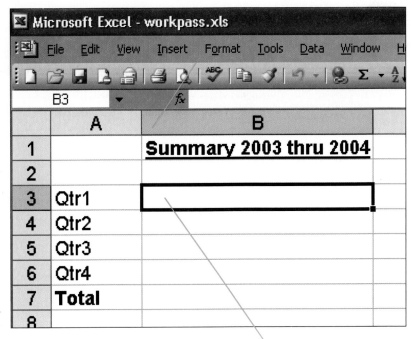

1 Create a new worksheet then select the cell you want to link

2 Type in the formula sequentially according to these rules:

- Type =
- Type in the reference to the cell on the first worksheet
- Type in the relevant operator – in this case, +
- Type in the reference to the cell on the second worksheet
- Press Enter

In our specific example (and given that the 2003 totals are on Sheet11 and the 2004 totals on Sheet12), the formula will be:

=Sheet11!B3+Sheet12!B3

Links between workbooks

Excel has no formal procedure for finding links. However, there are 2 effective work-arounds.

To locate links, close all source files then search for square brackets (and set the Look in: value to Formulas). See page 149 for more information.

Alternatively, since links are used in names, look in the Refers to box in the Define Name dialog (Insert, Name, Define): workbooks are shown in square brackets.

You can also insert links to other workbooks, either open or on disk. Look at the illustration below:

	A	B
1		
2	2002	=SUM('C:\Workbooks\[2002_Sales.xls]Sheet11'!B3)
3	2003	=SUM([2003_Sales.xls]Sheet12!B3)
4	2004	=Sheet2!B4
5		
6	Three Year Total	=SUM(B2:B4)
7		
8		

This is an excerpt from a new workbook: "2004_Sales.xls". This, as its name implies, totals sales for the years 2002 thru 2004. The formula in B2 is:

=SUM('C:\Workbooks\[2002_Sales.xls]Sheet11'!B3)

Here, we're instructing Excel 2003 to refer to a workbook called "2002_Sales.xls" in the "Workbooks" folder. This workbook isn't currently open. Notice that:

You can have cell references in formulas include worksheet names by separating the name and reference with "!" (but omit the quote marks).

For example, to refer to cell "A18" in worksheet "12", type: Sheet12!A18 within the formula.

- the full address is enclosed in single quotes

- the workbook title is surrounded by square brackets

Study the formula for B3 below:

=SUM([2003_Sales.xls]Sheet12!B3)

Here, we don't need to specify the workbook address (i.e. the drive and folder) because the file is already open. Apart from this, however, the same syntax applies.

And the formula for B4:

=Sheet2!B4

This formula refers to a specific worksheet and cell within the current workbook ("2004_Sales.xls") using the standard techniques we've discussed in earlier chapters.

You can link to workbooks (but not those in HTML format) on intranets or the Web. Copy the data you want to link to. In a new worksheet, choose Edit, Paste Special. Click Paste Link.

3D references

In the example discussed on pages 130 and 131, all the worksheets have exactly the same format: each quarterly amount lies in the same cell on each sheet. When this is the case, you can use an alternative method of summarizing the sales figures on the third sheet: 3D referencing. Using 3D references is often quicker and more convenient.

3D references consist of both of the following:

- a sheet range (i.e. the beginning and end sheets are specified, separated by a colon)

- a standard cell range

Entering a 3D reference

Not all Excel functions support 3D referencing. Those that do include Average, Count, Max, Min and Sum.

1 Select a cell

2 Type in the formula sequentially according to these rules:

- Type =
- Type in the appropriate function then (
- Type in the reference to the first worksheet, followed by a colon
- Type in the reference to the final worksheet
- Type !
- Type in the cell range in the normal way, then)
- Hit Enter

You can't use the intersection operator in 3D referencing.

In our specific example (and given that the 2002 totals are on Sheet11 and the 2003 totals on Sheet12, both in cell B3), the 3D formula will be:

=Sum(Sheet11:Sheet12!B3)

Comparing workbooks

You can display workbooks side by side, for comparison purposes.

I   With more than one workbook open, choose Window, Compare Side by Side with...

If several workbooks are open, after step 1 select the one you want to compare.

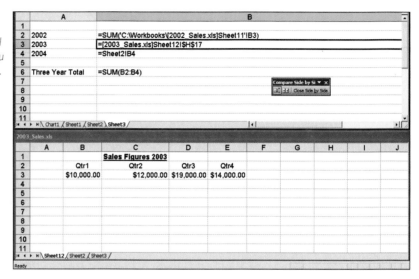

Using the Compare Side by Side toolbar

I   Select this to scroll thru both workbooks simultaneously – cool, huh?

3   Click here to revert to the previous view

2   Workbooks lost their original position? Click this to restore the windows to the position they occupied when you started comparing

Outlining

Outlines use levels (up to 8) to allow you to expand or collapse sections of a worksheet at will, and are nested (each inner level supplies details of the earlier outer one).

An alternative way to hide rows or columns temporarily is to outline (or group) them. When you apply outlining to specific data within a worksheet, Excel 2003 inserts an Outline Level bar against it. You can then specify whether the data displays or not.

Applying outlining

| | Select a cell range

2 | Pull down the Data menu and click Group and Outline, Group

3 | Below, rows 3–6 have been outlined and will be hidden – note the row and column Level bars (see over for how to use them)

Before you create an outline, ensure that the following conditions are met:

- *the data is in a range*
- *each column has a label in the first row and contains similar information*
- *the rows are together*
- *summary rows are present above or below each group of detail rows*
- *there are no blank rows or blank columns*

Here, the range F3:F6 has also been grouped.

To hide the Outline Level bar(s), choose Tools, Options. Activate the View tab and deselect Outline symbols. Click OK.

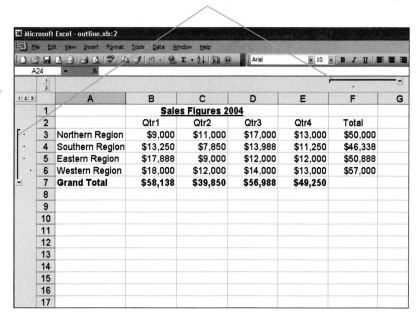

4 | You can apply an automatic outline when:

- summary formulas refer to the detail data
- all the columns with summary formulas are to the left or right of detail data

5 | Select cells then choose Data, Group and Outline, Auto Outline

Hiding/unhiding outlined data

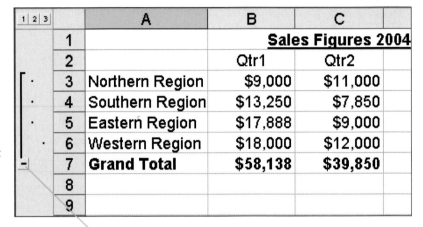

You can apply automatic styles to outlines. Select the relevant cells. Choose Data, Group and Outline, Settings. Check Automatic styles then click Apply styles.

1 To hide outlined data, click here (to display it again, click the + box)

2 Use the same technique with the column level bar

3 Alternatively, refer to the outline symbols (if they aren't there, choose Tools, Options. Select the View tab and check Outline symbols). Click the smaller number(s) to hide data, the larger numbers to reveal it

Removing outlines

1 Make a selection which includes the appropriate row(s) or column(s)

2 Here, rows 3 thru 6 have previously been outlined and are currently hidden; to remove this outlining, cells A2:E7 have been selected (selecting rows 2 thru 7 would produce an error)

You can hide data without using outlining. Select the row(s) or column(s) to be hidden. Choose Format, Row, Hide or Format, Column, Hide.

To unhide data, make a selection which includes the row(s) or column(s). Choose Format, Row, Unhide or Format, Column, Unhide.

You can partially remove outlines. Shift+click the [+] or [–] for the group then follow steps 3 thru 4.

You can change an outline's direction. Choose Data, Group and Outline, Settings then set new Direction options.

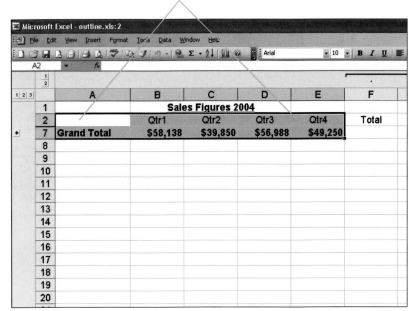

3 Pull down the Data menu and click Group and Outline, Ungroup

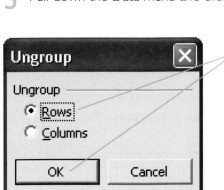

4 Make the relevant selection and confirm

Splitting worksheets

Pre-selecting a row or column inserts 1 Split bar and 2 panes.

Excel 2003 has two further techniques you can use to make complex worksheets easier to understand.

Splitting worksheets

1   Select the row or column before which you want the worksheet to be split, or simply select one cell for a double split (as below)

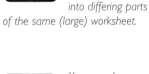

Splitting is especially useful when you want to paste information into differing parts of the same (large) worksheet.

2   Pull down the Window menu and click Split

3   Here, a single cell in column D was selected before step 1 was performed; as a result, Excel has inserted two Split bars and created four panes

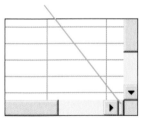

You can also create splits by dragging on the Split bar at the top of the vertical scroll bar or on the right of the horizontal scroll bar.

	A	B	C	D	E	F	G	H	I	J	K	L	M
1													
2		Video Rentals				Rental			Net Profit				
3						Price			Number of Rentals				
4		Rental Price=		$2.50		$400.00	100	125	150	175	200		
5		Number of Rentals=		200		$1.00	$0.00	$25.00	$50.00	$75.00	$100.00		
6		Total Income=		$500		$1.25	$25.00	$56.25	$87.50	$118.75	$150.00		
7						$1.50	$50.00	$87.50	$125.00	$162.50	$200.00		
8		Total Costs=		$100		$1.75	$75.00	$118.75	$162.50	$206.25	$250.00		
9						$2.00	$100.00	$150.00	$200.00	$250.00	$300.00		
10		Net Profit=		$400		$2.25	$125.00	$181.25	$237.50	$293.75	$350.00		
11						$2.50	$150.00	$212.50	$275.00	$337.50	$400.00		
12													
13													
14													
15													
16													
17													
18													
19													
20													
21													
22													
23													
24													
25													
26													
27													
28													

4   With horizontal splits, dragging either scroll box on the right of the screen moves the respective pane (but not the other) up or down. Dragging the horizontal scroll box, however, moves both panes to the right or left

5   With vertical splits, the vertical scroll box moves both panes while the horizontal scroll boxes are pane-specific

Freezing worksheets

Freezing panes prevents their data from scrolling and running away with you.

Use freezing when you need to keep column or row labels visible while you scroll thru data.

Freezing and splitting are mutually exclusive.

1 To create 2 panes with the top pane frozen, select the row above which you want the split inserted

2 To create 2 panes with the left pane frozen, select the column to the left of which you want the split inserted

3 To create 4 panes with the upper and left panes frozen, select the cell to the right of, and below, where you want the split

4 Finally, choose Window, Freeze

	A	B	C	D	E	F	G	H	I	J	K
1											
2		Video Rentals				Rental			Net Profit		
3						Price			Number of Rentals		
4		Rental Price=		$2.50		$400.00	100	125	150	175	200
5		Number of Rentals=		200		$1.00	$0.00	$25.00	$50.00	$75.00	$100.00
6		Total Income=		$500		$1.25	$25.00	$56.25	$87.50	$118.75	$150.00
7						$1.50	$50.00	$87.50	$125.00	$162.50	$200.00
8		Total Costs=		$100		$1.75	$75.00	$118.75	$162.50	$206.25	$250.00
9						$2.00	$100.00	$150.00	$200.00	$250.00	$300.00
10		Net Profit=		$400		$2.25	$125.00	$181.25	$237.50	$293.75	$350.00
11						$2.50	$150.00	$212.50	$275.00	$337.50	$400.00
12											
13											
14											
15											
16											
17											
18											
19											
20											
21											
22											
23											
24											
25											
26											

Sheet9 / Sheet8 / Sheet7 / Sheet16 / Sheet3 /

ready

5 Here, selecting Column E before the worksheet was frozen has created a vertical freeze. Dragging the horizontal scrollbar moves only the right-hand pane to the left or right but has no effect on the left-hand pane. The effect of dragging the vertical scroll bar is unchanged (both panes move up or down). This situation is reversed for horizontal freezes

Adjusting worksheet splits

Redefining a split

	A	B	C	D	C	D	E
1							
2		**Video Rentals**			ntals		
3							
4		Rental Price=		$2.50	ce=	$2.50	
5		Number of Rentals=		200	Rentals=	200	
6		Total Income=		$500	ne=	$500	
7							
8		Total Costs=		$100	s=	$100	
9							
10		Net Profit=		$400		$400	
11							
12							
13							
14				╫			
15							
6		Total Income=		$500	ne=	$500	
7							
8		Total Costs=		$100	s=	$100	
9							
10		Net Profit=		$400		$400	

Drag the Split Bar to a new location (but not in frozen worksheets)

2 Drag where the split bars intersect to move both bars

Removing a split

Double-click each split bar (but not in frozen worksheets). Or pull down the Window menu and select Remove Split

Unfreezing a worksheet

Pull down the Window menu and click Unfreeze Panes

Formatting and research

Worksheets look and work a lot better when they're formatted intelligently. In this chapter, you'll learn to customize cell formatting. You'll specify how cell contents align, apply fonts and type sizes and border cells. You'll also fill cells, format data automatically with AutoFormats and transfer formatting between cells via Format Painter. Then you'll use conditional formatting to have Excel flag cells which meet specific criteria. You'll also carry out data searches/substitutions and use text styles to make formatting even easier.

Finally, you'll carry out spell-checks and use the Research Task Pane to look up synonyms, translate text and carry out research on the Web.

Covers

Chapter Twelve

Cell alignment and text wrap

By default, Excel aligns text to the left of cells, and numbers to the right. However, you can change this and other alignment aspects.

1 Select the cell(s) whose contents you want to realign then hit Ctrl+1

2 Ensure the Alignment tab is active

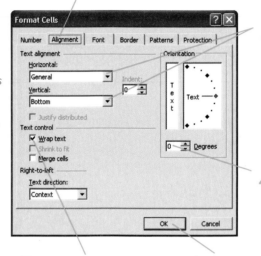

3 Select vertical and horizontal alignments and, optionally, insert a value in Indent to indent cell contents (by character widths)

4 Enter a rotation angle

5 Check this to wrap text – see below

6 Click here

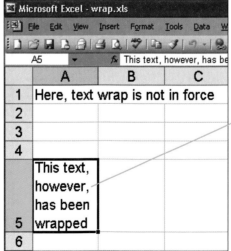

Text wrap forces surplus text onto separate lines within the host cell (instead of overflowing into adjacent cells to the right) and makes text look neater and easier to follow

Changing fonts and styles

Excel lets you carry out the following actions on cell contents (numbers and/or text). You can:

Don't overdo formatting changes; use them in moderation, to make your worksheets more impactful.

- apply a new font and/or type size

- apply a font style (for most fonts, you can choose from: Regular, Italic, Bold or Bold Italic)

- apply a color

- apply a special effect: <u>underlining</u>, ~~strikethrough~~, superscript or subscript

Amending the appearance of cell contents

1 Select the cells you want to format then hit Ctrl+1

2 Carry out step 3 below. Now follow any of steps 4–7, as appropriate. Finally, carry out step 8

Check Normal Font to apply the default formatting.

3 Ensure the Font tab is active

5 Type in a type size

To apply underlining, click the arrow to the right of the Underline box and select an underlining type.

6 Specify a color

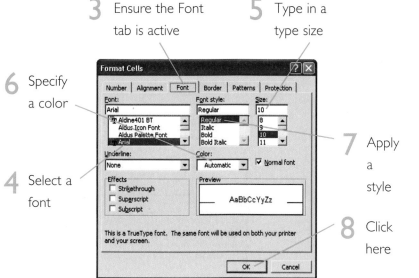

4 Select a font

7 Apply a style

To apply a special effect, click any of the options in the Effects section.

8 Click here

Bordering cells

Excel 2003 lets you define a border around:

- the perimeter of a selected cell range

- specific sides within a cell range

You can customize the border by choosing from a selection of pre-defined border styles. You can also add new line styles to specific sides, or color the border.

You can also border by hand. In the Borders toolbar (View, Toolbars, Borders), set the style and color. Then click this button:

and drag out a border.

Applying a cell border

1 Select the cells you want to border then hit Ctrl+1

2 Carry out step 3 below. Follow step 4 to apply an overall border. Carry out step 5 if you want to deactivate one or more border sides. Perform step 6 if you want to color the border. Finally, carry out step 7

3 Ensure the Border tab is active

If you want to customize the border style, apply a line style from the Style section just before step 4.

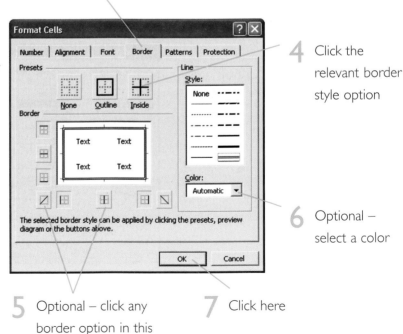

4 Click the relevant border style option

6 Optional – select a color

5 Optional – click any border option in this section to deselect it

7 Click here

Shading cells

You can only apply a foreground color if you apply a foreground pattern as well.

Excel 2003 lets you apply a background color, a foreground pattern or a foreground color to cells. Interesting effects can be achieved by using pattern and color combinations with colored backgrounds.

Applying a pattern or background

First, select the cell range you want to shade. Pull down the Format menu and click Cells. Now carry out step 1. Perform step 2 to apply a background color and/or 3–5 to apply a foreground pattern or a pattern/color combination. Finally, follow step 6.

| Ensure the Patterns tab is active

Use this handy shortcut. When you want to apply the most recently used color, click this button on the Formatting toolbar.

Or click the arrow and select another color in the list. (To remove a fill, hit No Fill instead.)

3 Click here to apply a foreground pattern or a pattern/color combination

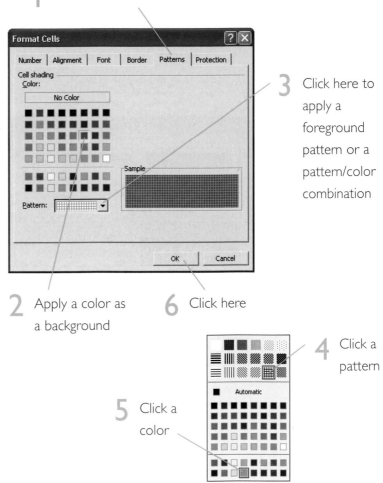

Use borders, colors and patterns to distinguish between different types of information and thus make your worksheets easier to understand.

2 Apply a color as a background

6 Click here

4 Click a pattern

5 Click a color

AutoFormat

Excel 2003 provides a shortcut to the formatting of worksheet data: AutoFormat. AutoFormat consists of some 16 pre-defined formatting schemes. These incorporate specific excerpts from the font, number, alignment, border and shading options discussed earlier. You can apply any of these schemes to selected cell ranges with just a few mouse clicks. You can even specify which scheme elements you don't wish to use.

AutoFormat works with most arrangements of worksheet data.

Using AutoFormat

To remove an AutoFormat, select the None format at the bottom of the list.

Format cell ranges or series (lists) with AutoFormat.

1 Select the cells (more than one) you want to format then choose Format, AutoFormat

2 Select an AutoFormat

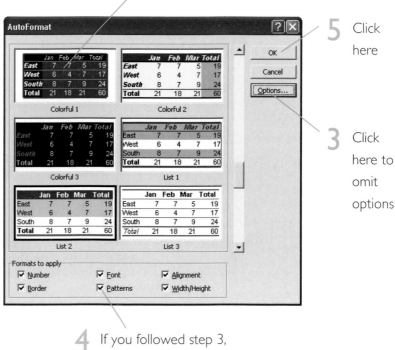

5 Click here

3 Click here to omit options

4 If you followed step 3, uncheck options you don't want to use

The Format Painter

Excel 2003 provides a very useful tool which can save you a lot of time and effort: the Format Painter. You can use the Format Painter to copy the formatting attributes from cells you've previously formatted to other cells, in one operation.

Using the Format Painter

1 Apply the necessary formatting, if you haven't already done so. Then select the formatted cells

Double-click the Format Painter icon if you want to apply the selected formatting more than once. Then repeat step 3 as often as necessary.

You can also use Format Painter with "objects" (e.g. pictures or clip art).

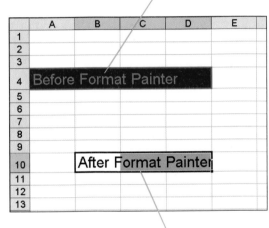

2 Refer to the Standard toolbar and click this icon:

3 Select the cell(s) you want the formatting copied to

4 The end result

5 Press Esc when you've finished using Format Painter

Conditional formatting

You can apply conditional formats to cells. Conditional formats are formatting attributes (e.g. color or shading) which Excel imposes on cells when the criteria you set are met. Conditional formats help you identify cells and monitor worksheets.

For instance, if B10 is the total of the number of videos rented out, you could tell Excel to make B10 red if the value it contains falls below a certain level, or blue if it exceeds it . . .

Applying conditional formatting

To add more than 1 condition, click Add then repeat steps 2 thru 7.

1 Select a cell range then choose Format, Conditional Formatting

You can use a TRUE/FALSE formula to define the match. Click here and select Formula Is. Now type the formula in the field to the right.

2 Click here; select a comparison phrase

3 Type in 1 or more match values

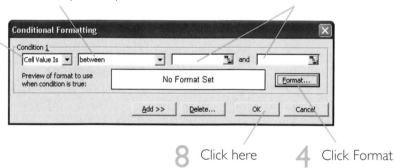

8 Click here   4 Click Format

To find conditional formatting, press F5. Click Special. Select Conditional formats, then All to find any conditional formatting or Same to find cells with the same conditional formatting. Click OK.

5 Activate a tab

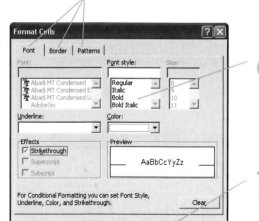

6 Select formatting options

7 Click here

Formatting which alters cell size (e.g. font changes) can't be used as a conditional format. As a result, these options are grayed out in the Format Cells dialog.

Find operations

You can use wildcards in your searches (but not in replace operations). However, the only Excel wildcards are:

- ? stands for any one character
- * stands for any number of characters
- ~ prefix this to ? or * (if you want to search for these characters rather than use them as wildcards)

Excel 2003 lets you search for and jump to text or numbers (in short, any information) in your worksheets. This is a particularly useful feature when worksheets become large and complex.

You can organize your search by rows or by columns. You can also specify whether Excel looks in:

- cells that contain formulas – **follow step 3 and select Formulas in the Look in box**

- cells that don't contain formulas – **follow step 3 and select Values in the Look in box**

Additionally, you can insist that Excel only flag exact matches (i.e. if you searched for "11", Excel would not find "1111"), and you can also limit text searches to text which has the case you specified (e.g. searching for "PRODUCT LIST" would not find "Product List" or "product list").

Searching for data

To search for data over more than one worksheet, select the relevant sheet tabs before launching the Find dialog box.

1 To search the entire worksheet, hit Ctrl+F

If you want to restrict the search to specific cells, select a cell range before you initiate a search.

2 Type in the data you want to find

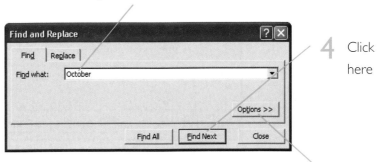

4 Click here

You can also search for specific formatting (such as typefaces, alignments and borders). After step 3, click Format and complete the Find Format dialog.

3 To specify the search direction, limit it to certain cell types or make it case-specific, click Options and complete the dialog which appears

Find-and-replace operations

When you search for data, you can also have Excel 2003 replace it with something else.

Find-and-replace operations can be organized by rows or columns. However, unlike straight searches, you can't specify whether Excel looks in cells that contain formulas or not. As with straight searches, you can, however, limit find-and-replace operations to exact matches and also (in the case of text) to precise case matches.

Normally, find-and-replace operations only affect the host worksheet. If you want to carry out an operation over multiple worksheets, pre-select the relevant sheet tabs.

Running a find-and-replace operation

1 Select a range if you want to restrict the operation to this

2 Hit Ctrl+H

3 Type in the data you want to find

4 Type in replacement data

5 To set options (see step 3 on page 149) click here

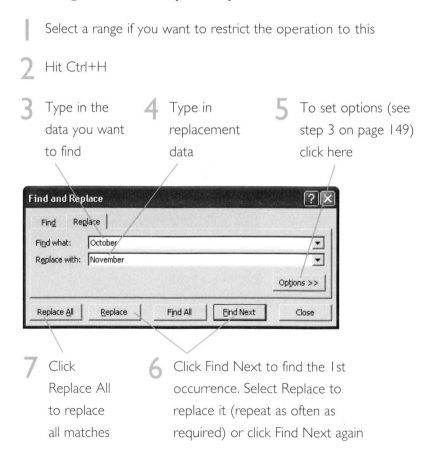

7 Click Replace All to replace all matches

6 Click Find Next to find the 1st occurrence. Select Replace to replace it (repeat as often as required) or click Find Next again

Spell-checking

You can customize spell-checking (for example, you can specify which language is used or whether Excel checks capitals or words with numerals). Choose Tools, Options and hit the Spelling tab.

Spell-checking your worksheet

When you've initiated a spell-check, Excel flags it and produces a special dialog (see below) when it encounters a word or phrase it doesn't recognize. Usually, it provides alternative suggestions; if one of these is correct, you can opt to have it replace the flagged word. You can do this singly (i.e. just this instance is replaced) or globally (where all future instances – within the current checking session – are replaced).

Alternatively, you can have Excel ignore *this* instance of the flagged word, ignore *all* future instances of the word or add the word to its internal dictionary. After this, Excel resumes checking.

Excel 2003 replaces some words/phrases automatically as you type (e.g. "accross" becomes "across"). This is called AutoCorrect.

To add your own substitutions, choose Tools, AutoCorrect Options. In the Replace field, insert the incorrect word; in the With field, type in the correct version. Click OK.

1 Pre-select cells if you want to restrict the check to them

2 Hit F7

3 If one of the suggestions here is correct, click it, then follow step 4

Click Add to Dictionary to have the flagged word stored in Excel's dictionary and recognized in future checking sessions. Or click AutoCorrect to have Excel substitute its suggestion for all future instances of the flagged word, as you type.

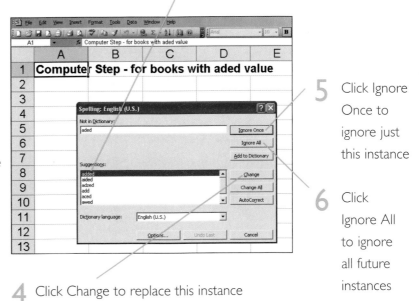

5 Click Ignore Once to ignore just this instance

6 Click Ignore All to ignore all future instances

4 Click Change to replace this instance

Searching for synonyms

Excel lets you search for synonyms while you're editing the active document. You do this by calling up Excel's resident Thesaurus. The Thesaurus categorizes words into meanings; each meaning is allocated various synonyms from which you can choose. The Thesaurus may also supply antonyms. For example, if you look up "good" in the Thesaurus, Excel lists "poor" as an antonym.

Using the thesaurus

1 Alt+click the word (but not in Edit mode) for which you want a synonym or antonym

2 Click here and select Thesaurus...

Antonyms have "(Antonym)" after their entries.

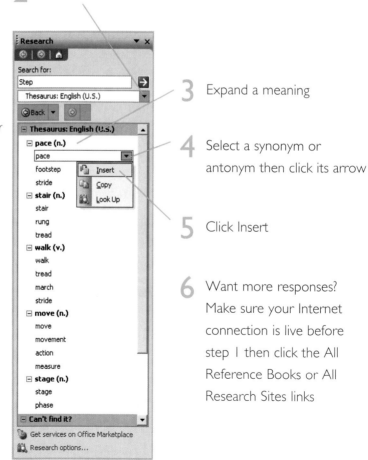

3 Expand a meaning

4 Select a synonym or antonym then click its arrow

5 Click Insert

6 Want more responses? Make sure your Internet connection is live before step 1 then click the All Reference Books or All Research Sites links

Translating text

Excel 2003 has a special Task Pane called Research. As we've just seen on the facing page, this incorporates a Thesaurus. However, it has a lot of other goodies as well, most or all of them online. Use the Research pane to find out all sorts of information. You can also use it to translate text into foreign languages.

Translating text

Be careful how much weight you attach to translation results. For example, "This cake is covered in nuts" translates in Italian as: "Questa torta è coperta in dadi". This is a bit hard to swallow since "dadi" means nuts (as in bolts).

1 With your Internet connection live, Alt+click once

3 Enter the text you want translated

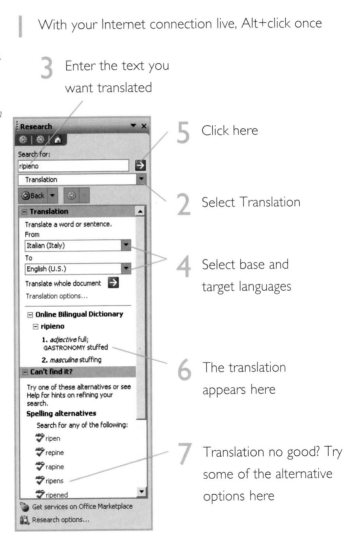

5 Click here

2 Select Translation

4 Select base and target languages

6 The translation appears here

7 Translation no good? Try some of the alternative options here

Carrying out research

We've already seen how the Research pane can be used to translate text. You can do a lot more with it than this, though.

| With your Internet connection live, Alt+click

3 Enter text you want to look up (as a general rule, try entering individual words or phrases and "building up" results)

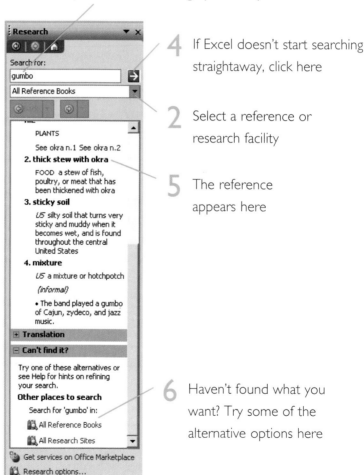

4 If Excel doesn't start searching straightaway, click here

2 Select a reference or research facility

5 The reference appears here

6 Haven't found what you want? Try some of the alternative options here

Styles – an overview

New workbooks you create have the following pre-defined styles as a minimum:

- Comma – *only includes numeric formatting (2 decimal places)*
- Comma (0) – *as above but 0 decimal places*
- Currency – *only includes numeric formatting (2 decimal places and the default currency symbol)*
- Currency (0) – *as above but 0 decimal places*
- Normal – *the default. Includes numeric, alignment, font and border/shading formatting (0 decimal places)*
- Percent – *only includes numeric formatting. Data is expressed as a percentage*

Styles are named collections of associated formatting commands. The cool thing about styles is that you can apply more than one formatting enhancement to selected cells in one go. Once a style is in place, you can change one or more elements of it and Excel 2003 applies the amendments automatically throughout the whole of the active workbook.

Creating a style

1 Apply the appropriate formatting enhancements to one or more specific cells and then select them

2 Choose Format, Style

3 Type in the new style's name

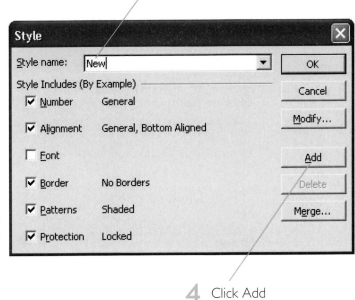

Keep styles simple. Select only single cells or cells with identical formatting. *(Styles aren't suitable for ranges of cells with different outline borders.)*

4 Click Add

5 When you're done using the Style dialog, click Close

6 Alternatively, follow steps 2 thru 3 then hit Modify. Use the Format Cells dialog to manually select the new style's formatting

Applying styles

Applying a style to formatted cells overrides the original formatting.

1 Select the cell(s) you want to apply the style to

2 Choose Format, Style

3 Click here; in the list, click the style you want to apply

Applying the Normal style to cells removes any attached style.

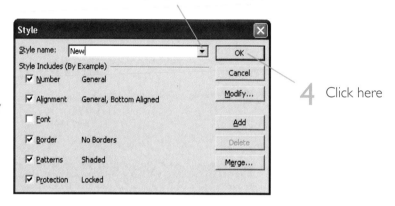

4 Click here

Shortcut for applying styles

Excel makes it even easier to apply styles if you currently have the Formatting toolbar (View, Toolbars, Formatting) onscreen.

By default, the Formatting toolbar doesn't display the Style box.

To make it visible, right-click any toolbar and click Customize. Select the Commands tab and select Format in the Categories column. Drag the boxed Style button in the Commands column onto the onscreen Formatting toolbar. Back in the Customize dialog, click Close.

1 Select the cell(s) you want to apply the style to

2 Click here

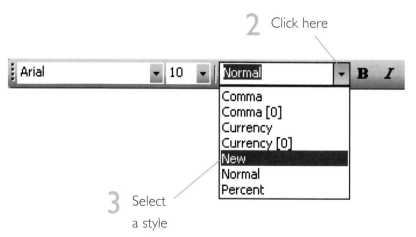

3 Select a style

Amending styles

1 Apply the appropriate formatting enhancements to one or more specific cells and then select them

	A	B	C	D	E
1					
2		Units used =	562		
3		Price per unit =	0.73		
4		Interest rate =	0.175		
5		Amount due excluding interest =	410.26		
6					
7					
8					
9					
10					
11					
12					
13					
14					

2 Choose Format, Style

3 Type in the name of the style you want to amend (just selecting it in the drop-down list doesn't work)

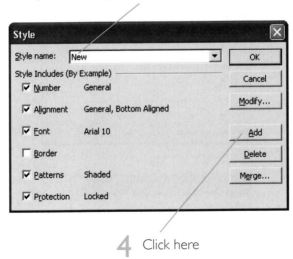

4 Click here

5 Click the Close button to apply the style change(s) to all examples of the style (but only in the current workbook)

Deleting and copying styles

Good housekeeping sometimes makes it necessary to remove unwanted styles from the active document. Excel 2003 lets you do this very easily.

Another useful feature is the ability to copy ("merge") styles from one workbook to another.

Deleting styles

1 Choose Format, Style

2 In the Style dialog, select a style in the Style name field. Click Delete – deletion is immediate and can't be undone

Copying styles

1 Open the workbook from which you want to copy styles, then the workbook you want to copy them into

2 Pull down the Format menu and click Style

When you get the styles you want into a workbook, consider saving it as template for future use – see page 55.

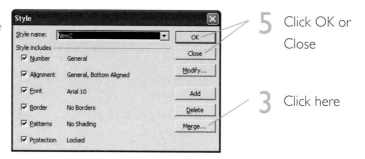

If the workbook you're copying from has styles with the same name as the target workbook, click Yes in the message to overwrite them or No to retain the originals.

5 Click OK or Close

3 Click here

4 Double-click the workbook which contains the styles you want to copy

Printing worksheets

With the size of many worksheets, successful printing rapidly becomes an issue. Fortunately, Excel 2003 lets you customize printed output with a very high level of precision.

In this chapter, you'll learn how to prepare your worksheets for printing. This involves specifying the paper size/orientation, margins and page numbering; inserting headers/footers (you'll also create your own designs); "autoscaling" output so it fits a given page width; using collation; and generally maximizing your use of space on the printed page. Then you'll use Print Preview mode to proof your worksheets and Page Break Preview to customize the printable area on-the-fly. Finally, you'll specify which worksheet components should be printed (and how) and define Print areas via a dialog route.

Covers

Chapter Thirteen

Page setup – an overview

Ensuring your worksheets print with the correct page setup can be a complex issue because, with the passage of time, worksheets become so large that they won't fit onto a single page.

You can customize a wide variety of page setup features. These include the paper size and orientation, the scale, the start page number and which worksheet components print. You can also set the standard margin settings.

Page Break Preview

Excel 2003 has a special view mode – Page Break Preview – which you can use to ensure your worksheet prints correctly.

There are 3 views you can use to make judgements about how your data will print:

- *Normal – use this to work with your data*
- *Print Preview (derives its settings from the current printer driver) – lets you see whether columns and margins need adjusting*
- *Page Break Preview – see on the right*

1 Pull down the View menu and click Page Break Preview

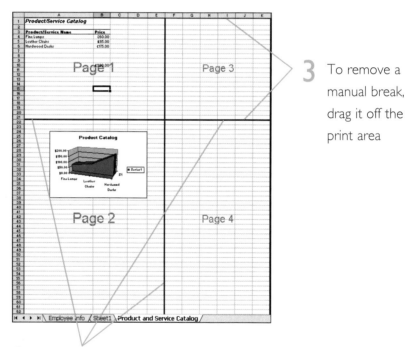

Page breaks you've inserted display as solid lines; breaks which Excel has inserted show as dotted lines.

3 To remove a manual break, drag it off the print area

To insert a manual page break, select the row or column immediately to the right of where you want the vertical or horizontal break to appear. Right-click and select Insert Page Break.

2 Drag page break margins to customize the printable area

4 To leave Page Break Preview, click Normal in the View menu

Setting worksheet options

Excel 2003 lets you:

The Page Setup dialog for charts in chart sheets has a special tab – see chapter 14 for how to use this.

- define a printable area onscreen
- define a column or row title which will print on every page
- specify which worksheet components should print
- print with minimal formatting
- determine the print direction

Using the Sheet tab in the Page Setup dialog

1 Choose File, Page Setup

You can print gridlines if you want – this may make data more readable. Just check Gridlines.

4 Include or exclude components

2 Select the Sheet tab

5 Type in the address of the row/column you want to use as a consistent title

If you want to print a specific cell range (print area), type in the address in the Print area field. Or click the box to the right of the Print area field and drag out a cell selection.

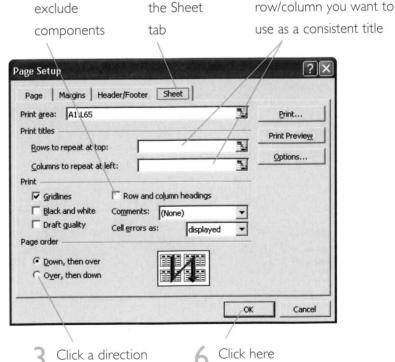

Check Draft quality for rapid printing with the minimum of formatting.

3 Click a direction

6 Click here

Setting page options

Excel comes with 17 pre-defined paper sizes which you can apply to your worksheets, in either portrait (top-to-bottom) or landscape (sideways on) orientation. This is one approach to effective printing. Another is scaling: you can print out your worksheets as they are, or you can have Excel shrink them so that they fit a given paper size (you can even automate this process).

Additionally, you can set the resolution and starting page number.

1 Choose File, Page Setup

To make your worksheet print in a specific number of pages, complete the "Fit to" fields.
   (Alternatively, enter "1" in the first field and leave the second blank to have Excel "autoscale" the worksheet so that it fits the paper width.)

Re step 5 – reducing the scaling percentage is a way of getting more data on the page (but check the font size in Print Preview before printing).

Select a print resolution in the Print quality box. This is measured in "dpi" (dots per inch) and is printer-specific.

2 Ensure the Page tab is active

3 Click the orientation you need

4 Select a paper size

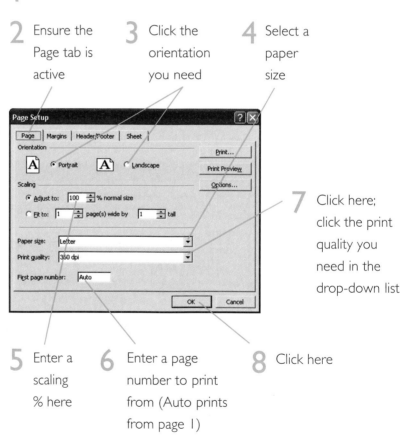

7 Click here; click the print quality you need in the drop-down list

5 Enter a scaling % here

6 Enter a page number to print from (Auto prints from page 1)

8 Click here

Setting margin options

Excel 2003 lets you set a variety of margin settings:

To view automatic page breaks, pull down the Tools menu and click Options. Activate the View tab. Ensure Page breaks is selected. Click OK.

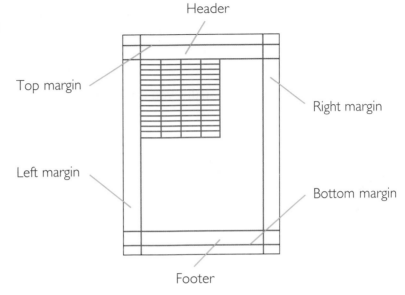

Header

Top margin

Right margin

Left margin

Bottom margin

Footer

Adjusting margin settings is one way to get more data on the page.

1 Choose File, Page Setup

2 Ensure the Margins tab is active

Enter values in the Header and Footer boxes to specify the distance to the top and bottom of the page respectively – these values should always be less than the Top and Bottom margin settings.

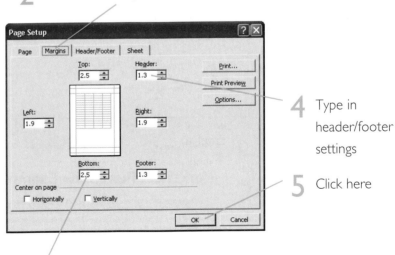

4 Type in header/footer settings

5 Click here

To specify how your worksheet aligns on the page, select an option under Center on page.

3 Type in the margin settings you need (they're previewed above)

Setting header/footer options

Excel 2003 provides a list of built-in header and footer settings. These settings include the title, the page number, the user's name or "Confidential".

1 Choose File, Page Setup

2 Ensure the Header/ Footer tab is active

3 Click here; select a header from the list

You can create your own headers and footers (for example, by specifying the font and alignment, inserting pictures and inserting file paths and names). Just click the Custom Header or Custom Footer button and complete the dialog.

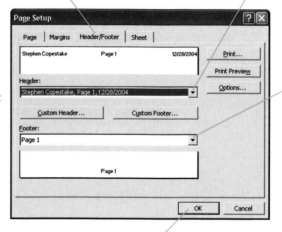

4 Click here; select a footer from the list

5 Click here

Headers and footers are only visible when printed or viewed in Print Preview.

6 One of the stock headers, viewed in Print Preview

Worksheet Functions   Confidential   Page 1

Worksheet Functions Examples

This worksheet contains sample formulas you can use to complete common spreadsheet tasks. Cells containing formulas are blue. To view a sample formula, hover your mouse cursor over the cell to display the comment. Or, press CTRL+` to switch between displaying values and displaying formulas on the worksheet. For more information about a worksheet function, select the cell containing the function, then click the Edit Formula (=) button on the Formula bar.

Suppressing the Display of Error Values

It is common for worksheet formulas to return an error value (#DIV/0!, #N/A, #VALUE!, #REF!, and # NUM!) if they are based on an unexpected value. An example is a simple division formula. If the source cell contains a zero, and #DIV/0! Error will be returned.

Using Print Preview

You can use a special view mode called Print Preview. This displays the active worksheet exactly as it will look when printed. Use Print Preview as a final check just before printing.

1 Pull down the File menu and click Print Preview

Print Preview toolbar

Excel's Print Preview mode only has two Zoom settings: Full Page and High-Magnification.

There are fewer toolbar options if you're previewing a chart.

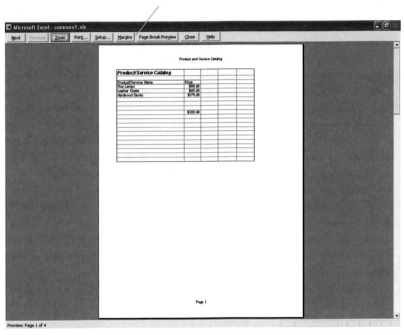

2 To zoom in or out, hit the toolbar Zoom button. Repeat to return to normal

3 Hit Setup in the toolbar to launch the Page Setup dialog

4 Hit Margins in the toolbar then reposition the onscreen margins

5 Hit Page Break Preview in the toolbar to see current breaks

6 Hit Next or Previous in the toolbar to view the succeeding or preceding page

Printing worksheet data

Excel 2003 lets you specify:

- the number of copies you want printed

- whether you want the copies "collated" (see the DON'T FORGET tip)

- which pages (or page ranges) you want printed

- whether you want the print run restricted to cells you selected before initiating printing

Collation is the process whereby Excel prints one full copy at a time. For instance, if you're printing three copies of a 10-page worksheet, Excel prints pages 1 thru 10 of the first copy, followed by pages 1 thru 10 of the second and so on. Collation is only enabled in multi-page worksheets.

Starting a print run

1 Select one or more worksheet tabs

You can print out your work with the current settings applying. This is a useful shortcut for proofing purposes. Just click this icon in the Standard toolbar:

2 Optionally, pre-select one or more cell ranges

3 Hit Ctrl+P

7 Type in a page range

4 Select a printer

6 Type in the number of copies required

To adjust your printer's internal settings before you initiate printing, click Properties then refer to your printer's manual.

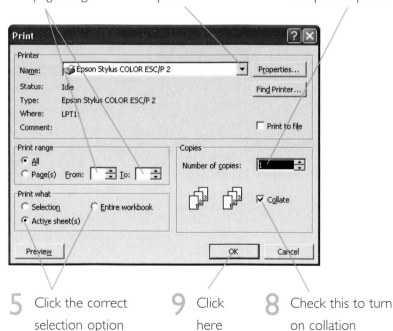

5 Click the correct selection option

9 Click here

8 Check this to turn on collation

Charts and graphics

Charts and other graphic elements make your worksheets more attractive and data more approachable, even fun.

In this chapter, you'll learn how to turn data into charts (both as objects within worksheets and as separate chart sheets) to make it more immediate and accessible. You're not stuck with the type of chart you allocate during the creation process: you can easily convert charts into other types. You can also save them to the Internet and intranets, interactively and non-interactively, then customize page setup issues so they print correctly. Another way you can spice up your worksheets is by adding pictures, from the Internet or via scanners and digital cameras. You can also insert AutoShapes, extraordinarily flexible graphic shapes, and add text to them.

Covers

Chapter Fourteen

Charting – an overview

Excel 2003 has comprehensive charting capabilities. You can have it convert selected data into its visual equivalent. To do this, Excel offers a wide number of chart formats and sub-formats.

You can create a chart:

- as a picture within the parent worksheet

- as a separate chart sheet (chart sheets have their own tabs in the Tab area and these operate just like worksheet tabs)

Preparing to create a chart

Before you create a chart, you have to ensure the data is arranged in the right way for the chart type you intend to use. Arrange the data you want to chart so it looks like the following:

Charts are linked to the originating data – if you amend the data, the chart is updated automatically.

When you create a chart, column/ row headings become axis or series names.

To make the edges of line charts less jagged, select a data series. Hit Ctrl+I. Select the Patterns tab and check Smoothed line. Click OK.

1 For Column, Line, Bar, Area, Surface or Radar charts, use either of these layouts:

Widgets	Nuts		Widgets	1 3
1	2		Nuts	2 4
3	4			

2 For simple pie charts, use 1 column of labels or 1 row of labels plus 1 row of data:

A 1		A	B	C
B 2		1	2	3

When you resize a chart, fonts rescale automatically, for more legibility.

3 For scatter or bubble charts, use 1 column each for x and y values:

X	Y
1	2
3	4

4 Need more detailed help with preparation? Enter "create a chart" in the Assistance Task Pane and hit Enter. In the list, select Create a Chart

Creating a chart

1 Select the cells you want to convert into a chart

2 Choose Insert, Chart

3 Click a chart type

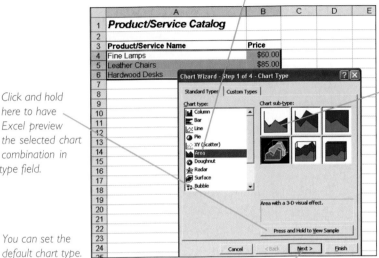

Click and hold here to have Excel preview the selected chart combination in the Chart sub-type field.

You can set the default chart type. Right-click a chart and select Chart Type. Hit the Standard Types tab then select a type and sub-type combination. Hit Set as default chart.

4 Click a chart sub-type

5 Click Next

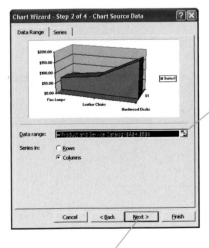

6 If you selected the wrong cells before launching the Wizard, click here to hide the dialog. Select another cell range then click:

7 Click Next

Click any of the additional tabs to set further chart options. For example, activate the Gridlines tab to specify how/ where gridlines display. Click Legend to determine where legends (text labels) display. Or click Data Labels for wide-ranging control over the content and formatting of data labels...

You can convert the whole of a 2D chart (or just a data series) to a new type. (With bubble and most 3D charts, though, you can only change the entire chart.)

Select the chart. Pull down the Chart menu and click Chart Type. Now follow steps 3 thru 5 on page 169.

Alternatively, you can apply a custom chart type. Launch the Chart Type dialog (as above). Activate the Custom Types tab. In the Chart type: field, click a custom type. Click OK.

To view an embedded chart in a separate window, select it then hit View, Chart Window.

8 Optional – name the chart and/or axes

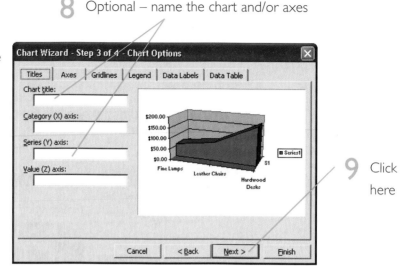

9 Click here

In the final dialog, you tell Excel whether you want the chart inserted into the current worksheet, or into a new chart sheet.

10 Click here to create a chart sheet

11 Or select an existing sheet

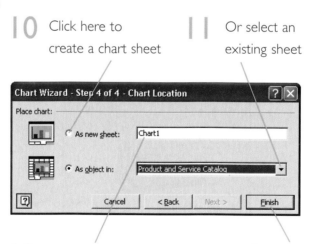

12 If you don't want to use the default chart sheet name, type in a new one here

13 Click here to generate the chart

Formatting charts

To amend the formatting of a chart component, do the following:

| Double-click the frame of the component you want to format

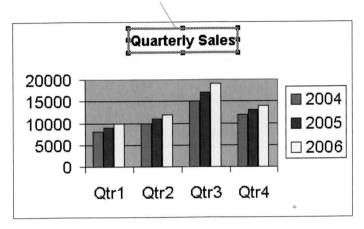

2 Activate the relevant tab

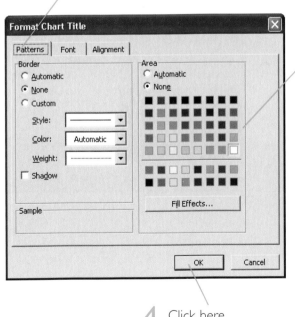

3 Complete the dialog (it varies with the component selected)

4 Click here

Downloading chart templates

Office Online has some handy chart templates that you can download and use, free-of-charge.

| With your Internet connection live, hit F1

2 Type in "charts" and click the arrow

3 Click a template link

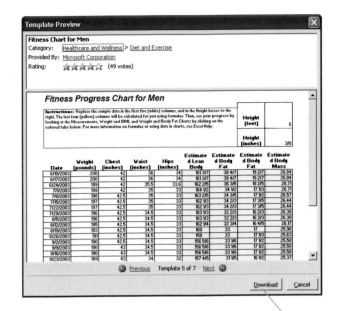

Want to see more chart templates? Hit the Previous or Next links.

4 Click here

5 Read the instructions. Here, enter details in the first 5 columns...

You can change a chart's location. Right-click a chart and select Location. Select As new sheet and type in a name for the new chart sheet or select As object in and pick an existing worksheet.

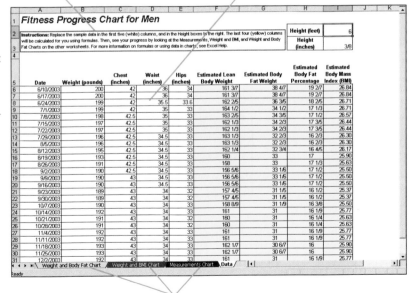

6 ...then view your progress in the ancillary worksheets

Page setup for charts

Most page setup issues for charts in chart sheets are identical to those for worksheet data. The main difference, however, is that the Page Setup dialog has a Chart (rather than a Sheet) tab.

In the Chart tab, you can opt to have the chart:

- printed at full size

- scaled to fit the page

- user-defined

You can also set the print quality.

You can specify where on the page an embedded chart prints by moving or resizing it in Page Break View. See page 160.

Using the Chart tab in the Page Setup dialog

1 Select a chart or chart tab then choose File, Page Setup

2 Ensure the Chart tab is active

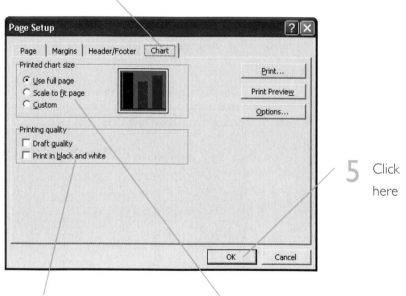

5 Click here

3 Click either option here to limit the print quality

4 Click a scale option (Custom ensures that, when you return to the chart sheet, you can adjust chart size with the mouse. The chart then prints at the size you set)

Saving charts to the Web

You can publish your charts (either as chart sheets, or as charts embedded in worksheets) to the Internet or intranets. This produces HTML files which can be viewed in more or less any browser, without the need to have access to Excel 2003. You can publish charts non-interactively or interactively.

(See page 58 for broad details of non-interactive v. interactive publishing.)

If you publish charts interactively, you may lose some formatting.

Publishing interactive charts

Select the relevant chart or chart sheet. Pull down the File menu and do the following:

1 Refer to (and implement where appropriate) steps 1 thru 7 on page 59 before you carry out the procedures discussed here (step 1 is especially important)

2 Select an embedded chart or chart sheet

3 Choose File, Save as Web Page

5 Click Publish

To save a chart non-interactively, select it. Carry out the relevant procedures on page 60 (but select Selection: Chart after step 1).

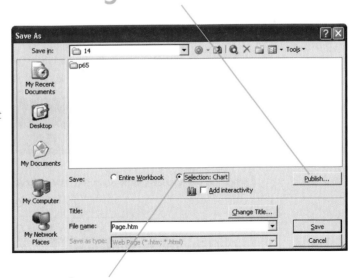

4 Select this

6 If applicable, specify which chart component you want to publish

7 Optional – specify a data item

8 Check this

9 Click here

11 Complete the Browse dialog

12 To preview your Web page in your browser, select Open published web page in browser

13 Click here

10 Name the published chart then hit OK

Re step 11 – use the Publish As dialog to select a destination folder and name the HTML file. (You can use it to save the file to a local network folder or to a Web/FTP folder.)

Check "AutoRepublish every time this workbook is saved" to have Excel automatically update your Web file each time you carry out a save operation. (Make sure you select the Refresh option in your browser when viewing.)

To work with interactively saved data, browser users must have the following:

- *Internet Explorer 4.1 or later*
- *an appropriate Microsoft Office license*

Inserting pictures

Inserting pictures via the Clip Art Task Pane

1 Click where you want to insert the picture

2 Select Insert, Picture, Clip Art

3 Enter one or more keywords (these help you find clips)

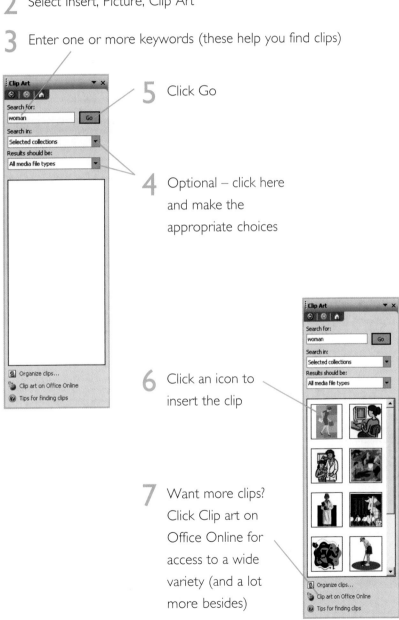

5 Click Go

4 Optional – click here and make the appropriate choices

6 Click an icon to insert the clip

7 Want more clips? Click Clip art on Office Online for access to a wide variety (and a lot more besides)

Inserting pictures – the dialog route

Once inserted into a worksheet, pictures can be resized and moved in the normal way.

1 Position the insertion point at the location within the active worksheet where you want to insert the picture

2 Select Insert, Picture, From File

4 Click here. In the drop-down list, click the drive/folder that hosts the picture

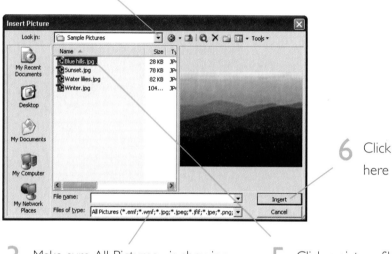

You can insert pictures or clips onto chart walls. First, select the chart wall then follow the procedures described on pages 177 thru 178.

6 Click here

3 Make sure All Pictures... is showing

5 Click a picture file

Inserting pictures via scanners or cameras

Want to customize the acquisition? Click Custom Insert instead then complete your device's dialog.

1 Select Insert, Picture, From Scanner or Camera

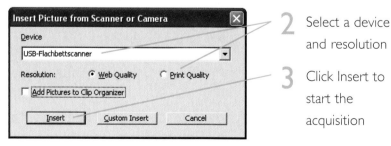

2 Select a device and resolution

3 Click Insert to start the acquisition

You can only import from TWAIN-compliant devices.

Using AutoShapes

AutoShapes represent an extraordinarily flexible and easy-to-use way to insert a wide variety of shapes into your worksheets.

Inserting an AutoShape

1 If the Drawing toolbar isn't onscreen, choose View, Toolbars, Drawing

3 Click an AutoShape category

4 Click an AutoShape

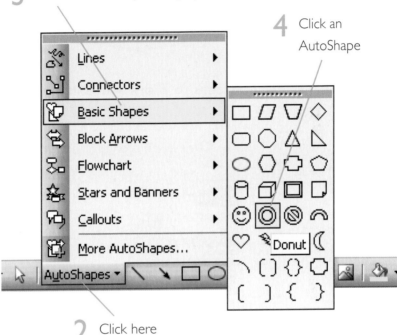

To change an AutoShape into another shape, select it. Click the Draw button in the toolbar. In the menu, select Change AutoShape. In the sub-menus, select a new category and shape.

2 Click here

5 Drag out the AutoShape (hold down Shift to maintain the original height/width relationship)

Adding text

Changes you make to an AutoShape also affect any inserted text.

1 Right-click the AutoShape and select Add Text. The insertion point appears inside the figure; type in the text. Click outside the AutoShape

Out of the box, AutoShapes can be a tad plain. To apply formatting (as here), right-click the AutoShape and select Format AutoShape. Complete the dialog box.

Resizing/rotating AutoShapes

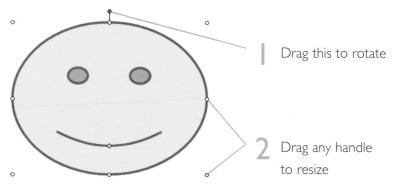

Drag this to rotate

2 Drag any handle to resize

You can make some AutoShapes 3D. Select the AutoShape then click this button in the toolbar:

In the menu, select a 3D shape (or select No 3-D to restore it to 2D).

You can also shadow AutoShapes: select the AutoShape then click the button to the left of the 3-D button. Select a shadow in the list.

Access to more AutoShapes

Ensure your Internet connection is live then click the AutoShape button on the Drawing toolbar

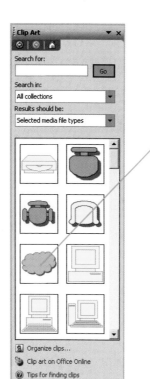

2 Select More AutoShapes in the menu

3 Drag an AutoShape into your worksheet

AutoShapes can function as hyperlinks. Select an AutoShape and hit Ctrl+K. Complete the dialog box.

Using macros

Automating simple or complex tasks you do oftentimes by recording them as macros can save you lots of time and effort.

This chapter shows you how to record tasks as macros and play them back whenever necessary. First, you'll learn how to set your macro security level, to prevent unauthorized macros from running when you open workbooks, then you'll master macro naming conventions. Finally, you'll go on to associate the macros you create with keystrokes, menu entries, toolbar buttons, graphics and hotspots, so they can be launched with just a few key presses or mouse clicks.

Covers

Chapter Fifteen

Recording a macro

Before you record a macro, you should ensure that your macro security level is not set to Very High or High (Tools, Macro, Security) if you want to run unsigned macros.

(Don't select Low unless your system is protected by up-to-date antivirus software.)

Excel 2003 lets you automate any task which you undertake frequently. You do this by recording it as a macro. A macro is a recorded series of commands which can be "rerun" at will. Using macros can be a real timesaver.

Once recorded, macros can be rerun:

- with the use of a special dialog

- by clicking a toolbar button

- by pressing a keystroke combination (defined when you record the macro)

- by clicking a special menu entry

- by clicking buttons, graphics or hotspots

Recording a macro

Here, we're recording a macro which will embolden and italicize cell contents in one operation (actions which can already be implemented separately by pressing Ctrl+B and Ctrl+I).

This is a very simple example, for the sake of clarity; however, you can easily record complex procedures as macros (in fact, that's the whole point of them).

1   Plan out (preferably on paper) the precise sequence of actions involved in the task you want to record

> **To make text bold and italic**
>
> 1. Click Format in Menu bar
>
> 2. Click Cells in menu
>
> 3. Select Bold/Italic in dialog box
>
> 4. Select OK

If you make an error when you record a macro, you can correct it in the Visual Basic Editor (Alt+F11) if you're a Visual Basic guru.

2   Choose Tools, Macro, Record New Macro

...cont'd

Re step 3 –macro names are subject to the following stipulations:

- *they must not be the same as cell names*
- *they must begin with a letter*
- *after the first letter, you can use letters, numbers and underlines (but not spaces)*

Re step 4 – Excel 2003 assumes you want the shortcut which will launch the macro to be: Ctrl+? where ? is any letter. However, you can also incorporate Shift into any keystroke combination; simply hold down one Shift key as you type in the letter.

Click the Relative References button in the toolbar if you want the macro to run relative to the position of the active cell.

Macros can't be undone.

Now carry out the following steps:

3 Name the macro

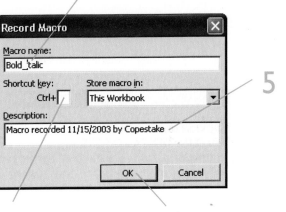

5 Optional – type in extra descriptive text

4 Optional – type in a launch keystroke

6 Click here

7 Perform the actions you want to record

8 When you're done, click this button in the toolbar

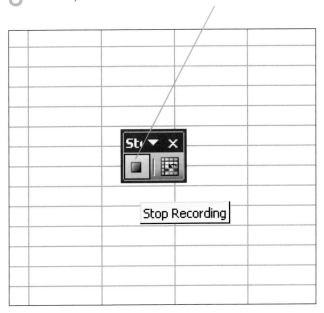

Running a macro

Launching macros via a dialog

1 Select the cells you want to apply the macro to

2 Hit Alt+F8

If you assigned a keyboard shortcut when you created a macro, hitting those keys is another great way to launch it.

3 Select a macro

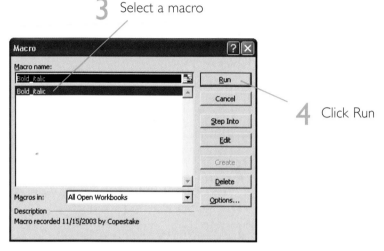

4 Click Run

To terminate a macro which is running, press Esc. In the Microsoft Visual Basic dialog, click End.

Launching macros via a menu

1 Select the cells you want to apply the macro to

2 Launch the menu you've added the macro to

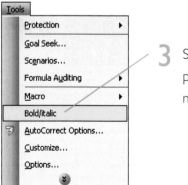

3 Select the macro entry (see page 186 for how to put macros on menus)

...cont'd

Launching macros via toolbars

| Select the cells you want to apply the macro to

Macros are touchy critters – everything has to be right for them to run correctly. If they're not (for example, if you search for italicized text when there isn't any), you'll get an error message.

2 Click here (this is the default macro toolbar icon)

Launching macros via hotspots

| Create an AutoShape for use as a hotspot then right-click it and select Assign Macro

Macros are a definite security issue – see the DON'T FORGET tips on pages 103 and 182.

2 In the Assign Macro dialog, double-click the macro you want to assign to the hotspot

3 With the graphic still selected, press Ctrl+1. Select the Colors and Lines tab. In the Fill/Color field, select No Fill; in the Line/Color field, select No Line. Click OK

You can use steps 1 thru 5 to assign macros to buttons or any other graphics, so that clicking them starts the macro.

4 Drag the graphic over another larger picture. As the fill and line color are set to none, the first graphic is invisible

5 Left-click the hidden hotspot (the cursor changes to a hand) to run the macro

Assigning macros to toolbars/menus

1   To assign a macro to a toolbar, make sure it's visible (View, Toolbars, *name of toolbar*)

2   Right-click any toolbar and select Customize

3   Select the Commands tab

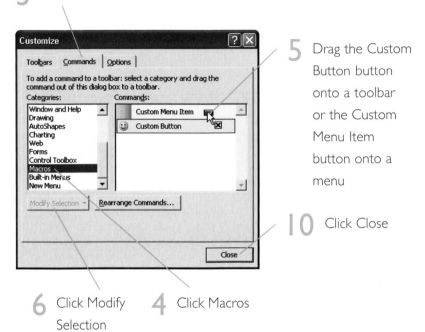

5   Drag the Custom Button button onto a toolbar or the Custom Menu Item button onto a menu

10   Click Close

6   Click Modify Selection

4   Click Macros

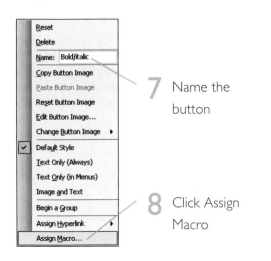

9   In the Assign Macro dialog, double-click a macro to assign it to the toolbar button/menu item

7   Name the button

8   Click Assign Macro

Index

D

E

Q

Quick File Switching   21

R

S

T